INTERNATIONAL TRENDS
IN
NATURE BASED TOURISM

INTERNATIONAL TRENDS IN NATURE BASED TOURISM

Anurag Fadia

CYBER TECH PUBLICATIONS
4264/3, Ansari Road, Daryaganj, New Delhi-110002 (India)
Ph.: 011-23244078. Fax: 011-23280028
E-Mail: cyberpublicationsdelhi@yahoo.com

International Trends in Nature Based Tourism

First Edition 2009

Published by G.S. Rawat

For Cyber Tech Publications

4264/3, Ansari Road, Daryaganj, New Delhi - 110 002

E-mail : cyberpublicationsdelhi@yahoo.com

Phone : 011-23244078,

Fax : 011-23280028

Printed at

Amit Enterprises, Moujpur, Delhi. Ph. - 9810878184

Preface

Natural tourism only accounts for a small fraction of the overall global tourist industry, it is reported to be one of fastest-growing tourism markets. Nature tourism's continued expansion offers opportunities to generate increased income and employment, both nationally and in remote rural areas, and to provide increased incentives for biodiversity conservation in state protected areas and on private lands.

Travel to natural areas which conserves the environment and sustains the will-being of local people. In other worlds it is a environmentally responsible and socially and entirely sound tourism. It is one of the effective means to finance conservation and alternative livelihood.

Aim of this book is to provide to our readers various aspects of the subject in proper perspectives. Effort has been made to cover important topics from the point of view of the course contents of universities and others institutions.

We acknowledge them all librarians and their staff members have been kind and helpful we thank them.

—Editor

Contents

Preface *v*

1. An Introduction to Nature Tourism 1

2. Evaluation and Monitoring of Ecotourism: Growth and Development 33

3. Nature Tourism and Environmental Impacts 68

4. Economic Impact of Nature Tourism and Cultural Activities in Worcester Country 87

5. Potential Development of National Parks in Indonesia 129

6. Sustainable Tourism in Protected Areas: Prospectus for Action for Scotland's National Parks 148

7. Nature Based Tourism and Parks 165

8. International Trends in Nature Tourism 207

9. Global Economic Impact of Ecotourism 218

Bibliography 255

Index 260

CHAPTER ONE

An Introduction to Nature Tourism

Nature tourism only accounts for a small fraction of the overall global tourist industry, it is reported to be one of the fastest-growing tourism markets. Nature tourism's continued expansion offers opportunities to generate increased income and employment, both nationally and in remote rural areas, and to provide increased incentives for biodiversity conservation in state protected areas and on private lands. These must be balanced with the risks of continued environmental degradation and greater pressure on protected areas, many of which lack the resources for effective management and are unprepared for significant growth in visitor numbers. Most of the economic benefits linked to tourist expenditures have so far been captured by commercial tourism operators in the richer countries (where most tourists originate) and in the larger cities of the host countries. This does little to support social and economic development in the remote rural areas where nature tourism destinations are located. Nature tourism has catalysed local or regional economic development in a few cases, but these have often been accompanied by negative environmental impacts from uncontrolled construction, as well as the abuse and overuse of destinations by inadequately regulated tour operators. Relatively few local communities have realised significant benefits from nature tourism on their own lands or in nearby protected areas.

Local communities' participation in nature tourism has been constrained by a lack of relevant knowledge and experience, lack of access to capital for investment, inability to compete with well-established commercial operations and simple lack of ownership rights over the tourism destinations. Nature tourism on privately-owned lands has in some cases been penalised by landowners' or residents' lack of effective tenure over wildlife and other natural attractions, or by policy distortions favouring land use alternatives such as agriculture, livestock or mining. Of course, these reservations are at least as applicable to many other private sector activities competing with tourism for land or other resources. From a conservation perspective, protected areas charging relatively low entry and use fees often supply the most valuable part of the nature tourism experience but capture little of the economic value of tourism in return.

While many governments have successfully increased tourist numbers by marketing their country's nature tourism destinations, most have not invested sufficient attention or resources in managing the natural assets which attract tourists or in the infrastructure needed to supper nature tourism. This has exposed sensitive sites of ecological of cultural value to the risk of degradation by unregulated tourism development, too manyvisitors and the impact of rapid immigration linked to new jobs and business opportunities. Despite these problems, the overall growth potential and some promising individual cases do suggest that nature tourism is an important sector where environmental conservation may effectively be combined with economic development in remote rural areas of developing countries on a meaningful scale. The policy-making priorities generally lie in four areas: (1) increasing and capturing more of the net economic benefits, (2) contributing more to local economic development, (3) mitigating environmental impacts, and (4) helping to finance biodiversity conservation (recognizing that only a small fraction of ecologically-important areas have the potential to attract significant tourism). Efforts to develop effective national policies for nature tourism have been frustrated by the lack of economic analysis of the options as well as the need to appreciated and reconcile the diverse stakeholder perspective. This indicates the need for applied economic research in selected case study countries which is not only targeted to provide usable insights but also sufficiently, grounded in an appreciation of the perspectives of the various stakeholders to produce results which are usable in cross-sectoral governmental decision-making. In other words, stakeholder involvement needs to be combined with technical analysis for policy development.

An overall menu of key research questions for evaluating options and strategies for optimising the economic and ecological benefits associated with nature tourism is identified. Country-specific policy research could prioritise from such a menu. In this volume and attempt has been made to examine various issues connected with nature based tourism. The focus is on concepts, structure and motivation, sources of finance, methods of monitoring and evaluation of this industry.

Finally a few guidelines for material such programmes successful both operators and entrepreneurs point of view are also discussed.

Nature tourism has grown as a consequence of the dissatisfaction with conventional forms of tourism which have, in a general sense, ignored social and ecological elements of foreign regions in favour of a more anthropocentric and strictly profit centred approach to the delivery of tourism products.

The analysis of ecotourism from the perspective of history, definition, and linkages to other related forms of tourism (i.e. adventure tourism and cultural tourism). A brief discussion of tourism typologies is offered as a means by which to understand better the documented differences that exist between ecotourist and other types of travellers. Until recently, there has been some confusion surrounding the etymology or origin of the term 'ecotourism', as evident in the tremendous volume of literature on the topic. For example, Orams (1995) and Hvenegaard (1994) write that the term can be traced back only to the late 1980s, while others (Higgins 1996) suggest that it can be traced to the late 1970s, through the work of Miller (see Miller 1989) on ecodevelopment.

One of the consistent themes emergent in the literature supports the fact that Ceballos-Lascurain was the first to coin the phrase in the early 1980s (see Thompson 1995). He defined it as 'travelling to relatively undisturbed or uncontaminated natural areas with the specific objective of studying, admiring, and enjoying the scenery and its wild plants and animals, as well as any existing cultural manifestations (both past and present) found in these areas' (Boo 1990: xiv). In an interview (van der Merwe 1996), Ceballos-Lascuain illustrates that his initial reference to the phrase occurred in 1983, while he was in the process of developing PRONAURA an NGO in Mexico. Recently, however, the term has been traced further back to the work of Hatzer (1965), who used it to explain the intricate relationship between tourists and the environments and cultures in which they interact. Hetzer identified four fundamental pillars that needed to be followed for a more responsible form to tourism. These included: (1) minimum environmental impact; (2) minimum impact on-and maximum respect for –host cultures; (3) maximum economic benefits to the host country's grassroots; and (4) maximum 'recreational' satisfaction to participating tourists. The development of the concept of ecotoruism grew, according to Hetzer (personal communication, October 1997), as a culmination of dissatisfaction with governments' and society's negative approach to development, especially from an ecological point of view. Nelson (1994) also adopts this particular stand in illustrating that the idea of ecotourism is in fact an old one, which manifested itself during the late 1960s and early 1970s, when researchers became concerned over inappropriate use of natural resources. Nelson suggests that the term 'eco-development' was introduced as a means by which to reduce such development.

In other related research, Fennell (1998) found evidence of Canadian government 'ecotours' which were operational during the mid-1970s. These ecotours centred around the Trans-Canada Highway and were developed on the basis of different ecological zones found along the course of the highway. The first of these encounters was developed in 1976. Based on the ecozone concept, they were flet to be rather progressive for the time despite the lack of a focused look at low impact, sustainability, community development, and the moral philosophy lebels that are attached to ecotourism in the 1990s.The ecotours were developed at a time when the Canadian government felt it important to allow Canadian and foreign travellers to appreciate the human-land relationship in Canada, through the interpretation of the natural environment. Although a set definition of ecotourism was not provided, each of the ecotour guides contains the following foreword:

Ecotours are prepared by the Canadian Forestry Service to help you, as a traveller, understand the features of the landscape you see as you cross the country. Both natural and human history are described and interpreted. The route covered by the Ecotours is divided into major landscape types, or Ecozones, and a map of each Ecozone shows he location of interesting features (identified by code numbers). While most features can be seen from your car, stops are suggested for some of them. Distances between points of interest are given in kilometers. Where side trips are described, distances are given to the turnoff from the highway. You will derive the maximum value from this Ecotour if you keep a record of the distance travelled and read the information on each point of interest before reaching it.

There seems to be universal acceptance of the fact that ecotourism was viable long before the 1980s in practice, if not in name. For example, Blangy and Nielson (1993) illustrate that the travel department of the American Museum of Natural History has conducted natural history tours since 1953. Probably the finest examples of the evolution of ecotourism can be found in the African wildlife-based examples of tourism developed in the early twentieth century and, to some, the nature tourism enterprises of the mid-nineteenth century (Wilson 1992). There are examples in the literature that illustrate that human beings, at least since the Romantic period, have travelled to wilderness for the intrinsic nature of the experience. Nash writes that during the nineteenth century many people travelled both in Europe and North America for the primary purpose of enjoying the outdoors, as illustrated in the following passage.

Alexis de Tocqeville resolved to see wilderness during his 1831 trip to the Untied States, and in Michigan Territory in July the young Frenchman found himself at last on the fringe of civilisation. But when he informed the frontiersmen of his desire to travel for pleasure into the primitive forest, they thought him mad. The American required considerable persuasion from Tocqueville to convince them that his interests lay in matters other than lumbering or land speculation.

Tocqueville was after something that we consider as

an essential psychological factor in travel: novelty. Nash (1982) credits the intellectual revolution in the eighteenth and nineteenth centuries as the push needed to inspire the belief that unmodified nature could act as a deep spiritual and psychological toinic. It required the emergence of a group of affluent and cultured persons who largely resided in urban environments to garnish this appreciation (e.g. Jean-Jacques Russeau and John Ruskin). For these people, Nash writes, 'wilderness could become an intriguing novelty and even a deep spiritual and psychological need.' In the United States, the sentiment at the time was not as strong as it was in Europe, where 'as late as the 1870s almost all nature tourists on the American frontier continued to be foreigners.'

When Americans did start travelling to the wild parts of their country it was the privileged classes that held the exclusive rights. A trip to Yellowstone in the 1880s, according to O'Gara (1996), was about three times as expensive as travel to Europe at the time. There was no question that those from the city were especially taken with Yellowstone's majesty, but their mannerisms left much to be desired, as evident in an account of such tourists.

Definitions of Ecotourism

Given the ambiguity associated with the historical origins of ecotourism, the purpose of the present section is to identify the key features, concepts, and principles of the term, especially the link between nature tourism (or nature-oriented tourism) and ecotourism. For example, Laarman and Durst, in their early reference to ecotourism, defined it as a nature tourism in which the 'traveller is drawn to a destination because of his or her interest in one or more features of that destination's natural history. The visit combines education, recreation and often adventure' (Laarman and Durst 1987: 5). In addition, these authors were perhaps the first to make reference to nature tourism's hard and soft dimensions, based on the physical regiour of the experience and also the level of interest in natural history. Laarman and Durst suggested that scientists would in most likelihood be more dedicated than casual in their pursuit of ecotourism, and that some type of ecotourist would be more willing to endure hardships than others in order to secure their experiences. The letter 'B' in Figure 3.1 identifies a harder ecotourism experience based on a more difficult or rigorous experience, and also based on the dedication shown by the ecotourist relative to the interest in the activity.

A subsequent definition by these authors (Laarman and Durst 1993) identifies a conceptual difference between ecotourism and nature tourism. In recognising the difficulties in defining nature tourism, they establish both a narrow and broad scope to its definition. Narrowly, they say, it refers to operators running nature-oriented tours; however, broadly it applies to tourism's use of natural resources including beaches and country landscapes. In their research they define nature tourism as 'tourism focused principally of natural resources such as relatively undisturbed parks and natural areas, wetlands, wildlife reserves, and other areas of protected flora, fauna, and habitats'. Given this perspective, there appears to be some consensus mounting in the literature that describes ecotourism as one part of a broader nature-based tourism. encompasses all forms of tourism—mass tourism, adventure tourism, low-impact tourism ecotourism—which use natural resources in a wild or undeveloped form—including species, habitat, landscape, scenery and salt and fresh-water features. Nature tourism is travel for the purpose of enjoying undeveloped natural areas of wildlife.

And conversely, that *ecourism* is low impact nature tourism which contributes to the maintenance of species and habitats either directly through a contribution to conservation and/or indirectly by providing revenue to the local community sufficient for local people to value, and therefore protect, their wildlife heritage area as a source of income.

Nature Tourism in Texas

Ecotourism in Texas provides an excellent example of how ecotourism is subsumed by nature tourism. In Texts, nature tourism is defined as 'discretionary travel to natural areas that conserves the environmental, social and cultural values while generating an economic benefit to the local community' (Texas Parks and Wildlife 1996: 2). Although hunting and fishing are reported to be traditional mainstays of nature tourism in Texas, the Task Force on Nature Tourism states that non-consumptive activities such as bird and wildlife watching, nature study and photography, biking, camping, rafting, and hiking have experienced the greatest growth over the past few years. In texas, the task force reports that tourism is the third largest industry in Texas, generating $23 billion annually, with the potential to replace oil and gas, and manufacturing as the highest income earner by the turn of the century.

The Great Texas Coastal Birding Trail is a key ecotourism attraction in the Lone Star State. The goal of this trail is to increase the opportunities for nature tourism in the coastal communities of Texas, in addition to conveying the value of conservation of people living in the region. Although the trail was conceived by the Texas Parks and Wildlife Department, it was made possible by transportation enhancement funds and the Texas Department of Transportation. The trail utilises existing transportation infrastructure (viewing platforms and boardwalks are being added on a continual basis) in creating recreational, economic, and educational opportunities for local people and tourists alike. Upon completion in 1998, it will comprise three main sections and span over 600 miles of coastline, incorporating some 300 birding stops in nine wildlife refuges, eleven state parks, one national seashore, and several city and country preserves.

Apart from the differences apparent in the work of Goodwin, some of the key variables or principles that separate ecotourism from its more broad-based nature counterpart include an educative component and a sustainability component, and the ethical nature of the experience. In view of the relationship between the two concepts, there does seem to be some merit in linking ecotourism to nature tourism, given the tremendous variety of nature-related tourism interests. However, there is also ambiguity in separating nature tourism from other forms of tourism, all of which rely upon the use of natural resources. Even mass, resort-based tourism relies upon undeveloped resources (i.e. beaches and the ocean) as a central component of the product and experience. An important aspect of Goodwin's discussion includes the fact that not all types of nature tourism are necessarily compatible with each other or the environment. Examples include hunting and bird- watching, which place different demands on the resource base, and users, and which have a different managerial focus (if managed at all) which is based on the consumptive nature of these activities. The importance of management in guiding the ecotourism product was central to the work of Fennell and Eagles (1990), who included the resource tour as the principal component of the ecotourism experience; the service industry, including tour operation, government policy, resource management, and community development; and the visitor experience, based on marketing, visitor management, and visitor attitudes. In their work, Fennell and Eagles recognised the value in management form the visitors' perspective, but also from the community and resource-based perspective (see also Hvenegaard 1994 of a good description of ecotourism conceptual frameworks).

The variability of approaches used to define ecotourism has quite naturally given way to many comprehensive approaches used to understand the term. In her approach to the concept, Ziffer (1989) acknowledges the variety of descriptive terms such as nature travel, adventure travel, and cultural travel, which are largely activity based; and also the value-laden terms such as responsible, alternative, and ethical tourism, which underscore the need to consider impacts and the consequences of travel. Ziffer feels that nature tourism, while not necessarily ecologically sound in principle, concentrates more on the motivation and the behaviour of the individual tourist. Conversely, ecotourism is much more difficult to attain owing to its overall comprehensiveness.

Like Ziffer's, the following definition by Wallance and Pierce (1996: 848) is also quite comprehensive, acknowledging the importance of a broad number of variables. To these authors, ecotourism is travel to relatively undisturbed natural areas for study, enjoyment, or volunteer assistance. It is travel that concerns itself with the flora, fauna, geology, and ecosystems of an areas, as well as the people (caretakers) who live nearby, their needs, their culture, and their relationship to the land it [*sic*] views natural areas both as home to nearby residents' specially. It is envisioned as a tool for both conservation and sustainable development—especially in areas where local people are asked to forgo the consumptive use of resources for others.

Wallance and Pierce suggest that this tourism may be said to be true ecotourism if it addresses six principles:

1. It entails a type of use that minimises negative impacts to the environment and to local people.
2. It increases the awareness and understanding of an area's natural and cultural systems and the subsequent involvement of visitors in issues affecting those systems.
3. It contributes to the conservation and management

of legally protected and other natural areas.

4. It maximises the early and long-term participation of local people in the decision-making processes that determines the kind and amount of tourism that should occur.

5. It directs economic and other benefits to local people that complement rather than overwhelm or replace traditional practices (farming, fishing, social systems, etc.).

6. It provides special opportunities for local people and nature tourism employees to utilise and visit natural areas and learn more about the wonders that other visitors come to see.

Both Ziffer and Wallance and Pierce recognise that for ecotourism to exist, it must strive to reach very lofty goals. By comparison, the Ecotourism Society advocates a much more general definiton of the term, one that advocates a 'middle-of-the-road' or passive position (see Orams 1995), and one which is more easily articulated. This organisation defines ecotourism as 'responsible' travel to natural areas which conserves the environment and improves the welfare of local people'. Preece *et al.* (1995) used the Australian National Ecotourism Strategy definition of ecotourism in their overview of biodiversity and ecotourism, which is also one that is quite general in nature. The strategy defines ecotourism an nature-based tourism that involves education and interpretation of the natural environment and is managed to be ecologically sustainable.

Although quite straightforward, these definitions level much to the interpretation of the reader. As identified in Table 3.1, definitions of ecotoruism over the years have emphasized different aspects of nature, relationships with local people, conservation and preservation, and so on. The main issue confronting researchers who are bent on structuring definitions is either to include a whole series of principles and variables related to the term, or to try to isolate specific variables which can be used to best represent the overall concept. The fact of the matter is that, either implicitly or explicitly, such variables or principles need to be more effectively used to observe, measure, and evaluate what is and what is not ecotourism.

In line with the previous discussion, Bottrill and Pearce (1995) point to the fact that the rich array of definition of ecotourism have done little to clarify its meaning. Instead they opt for a means by which to operationalise ecotourism through the development of a set of measurable key elements for participant, operators, and managers (see also Wallace and Pierce 1996, and their evaluation of ecotourism principles in Amazonas). In an analysis of 22 ecotourism ventures only five were classified as ecotourism using the following criteria; motivation (physical activity, education, participation), sensitive management, and protected area status. The authors submit that more work should follow to further define and modify the points and criteria raised. Their paper quite nicely addressed the need to more beyond definition to a position where ecotourism operators should be open to ethical and operational scrutiny by the public and other concerned stakeholders. This leads to the contentions of Miller and Kaye (1993: 37), who suggest that 'the merits of deficiencies of ecotourism...are not to be found in any label *per se*, but in the quality and intensity of specific environmental and social impacts of human activity in an ecological system.'

Some researchers have discussed the placing of time on determining whether tourists are ecotourists or not. For example, Ballantine and Eagles (1994) suggested that ecotourists could be defined on the basis of an intention to learn about nature, an intention to visit undisturbed areas, and a commitment of at least 33 per cent of their time to the first two criteria. Blamey (1995) sees some inherent problems with the implementation of such a measure. The time factor advocated by Ballantine and Eagles may be applicable in the safari ecotourism settings of African, but could be more problematic in less structured ecotourism settings and situations. For instance, Balmey asks if a ten-minute guided nature tour qualifies as a day ecotourism visit. Yet one can't help but grapple for acceptable definitions of ecoturism, as Ballantine and Eagles and others have done; the same has occurred with the meaning of 'tourism' in the past, and similarly for many other social science disciplines. While the tourism literature has seen fit to define; Tourism' under many different circumstances—time, space, economics, whole systems models-the same will likely occur for ecotourism. It depends on who is operationalising the concept, and for what purpose. (See also Buckley 1994).

Given the foregoing discussion, I have elected to provide my own definition of ecotourism. In light of the review of a significant number of definitions, it is based on what is felt to be the most important aspects of the phenomenon and on the need to be concise in including such principles. It is as follows: Ecotourism is a sustainable form of natural resource-based tourism that focuses primarily on experiencing and learning about nature, and which is ethically managed to be low-impact, non-consumptive, and locally oriented (control, benefits, and scale). It typically occurs in natural areas, and should contribute to the conservation or presentation of such areas.

Admittedly, this is more comprehensive than other definitions, but it strives to recognise that having been identified as a separate form of tourism, ecotourism must be classified and defined as such in order to maintain an element of homeogeneity. This feeling is not expressed without some hesitation based on the writing of some other authors who imply that most people who demand ecotourism want a softer, easily accessible, front-country type of experience (Kearsley 1997 in Weaver 1998) and that the 'popular' form of ecotourism demands mechanised transport, easy accessibility, and a high level of services (Queensland Draft Ecotourism strategy in Weaver 1998). The relationship between this very soft form of ecotourism and other types of tourism has not been fully examined. The belief in this book is that much more than simply demand must go into the understanding of ecotourism and ecotourists. In an attempt to stay clear this fine line, a harder stance on ecotourism is adopted. Furthermore, a stricter definition of ecotourism begs for the employment of measurable indicators in determining what is and is not ecotoruism. (See Orams 1995 for a description of the hard-soft path ecotourism continuum). An early example of this type of thinking can be seen through the efforts of Shores (1992), who identified the need for higher standards in the ecotourism industry through the implementation of a scale to measure the level of achievement according to the principles of ecotourism. The scale ranges from 0 (travellers made aware of the fragility of the environment in a general capacity) to 5 (a trip where the entire system was operating in an environmental way).

There reader will most certainly recognise the absence of culture as a fundamental principle of ecotourism in the aforementioned definition. This definition views culture only inasmuch as the benefits from ecotourism accrue to local people, recognising that culture, whether exotic or not, is part of any tourism experience. If culture was a primary theme of ecotourism then it would be cultural tourism. There is not doubt that culture can be part of the ecotourism experience; the point is, however, that it is more likely to be secondary motivation to the overall experience, no primary as in the case of nature and natural resources. For example, in a study completed by Funnell (1990) it was found that there was no statistically significant difference between the average Canadian traveller and ecotourists as regards many cultural attractions, including museums and art galleries, local festivals and events, and local crafts.

If one is to accept the fact that there currently exists an uneven base with which conceptually and empirically to determine differences in forms or types of nature tourists, it should thus be the task of researchers to focus on the isolation of variables by which to understand better the manifest and latent traits of these groups. Past research (see Bechert 1990) has combined education, experience, and learning into a comprehensive model of wilderness education. In this model learning is a key feature and is a variable which may also provide a basis from which to compare the one-site characteristics of the *nature tourism experience* over other familiar variables such as managements, culture, economics, and benefits. Other important variables to be considered (besides learning) may include the employment of skills or actions in the pursuit of the primary activity; the degree to which one subscribes to a strong or weak sense of what might be considered as 'biological' or 'preservationist affect' (the emotional tie that one has with plants, animals, or nature as a whole); and finally the degree of impact (consumptive to non-consumptive) caused by the type of tourism.

More specifically, learning relates to the need to gain knowledge on-site through interpretation and the information provided by guides and other facilitators. Further research in this area might endeavour to understand the differences or similarities between novelty and curiosity, and learning. In whale- watching, for example, many people just want to see a whale (novelty or curiosity), while conversely others want a more comprehensive learning-based whalewatching experience. In addition, future research may wish to examine the relationship between knowledge and learning in nature tourism. Knowledge can be thought of as information one applies to a situation, whereas learning is something that results from participation. There is little question that nature tourists learn from the experience, but it is important to view learning in terms of the primary motivation of the tourist. Second, skill may also be examined because it demonstrates that the application of skill if often employed at the expense of the environment rather than is some other benign fashion. Skill also relates to the previous discussion on primary motivation for participation in the nature tourism activity. There can be a strong case made for the assumption that ecotourism is learning based in its orientation, while other forms of nature tourism (e.g. mountain climbing) may be more skills based in their orientation. Third, biological affect may also provide some inroads in differentiating between nature tourists because it seeks to understand the perceptual place that flora, fauna, geological features, etc. occupy in the mind of the tourist. Consequently, the feelings of such users may dictate the forms of recreation participated in, and the effects of such activities on the natural world. This type of thinking relates to the work of Kellert (1985) on the attitudes of people towards animals on the basis of nine variables (negativistic and dominionistic as the most negative attitudes, versus naturalistic and ecologistic as the most positive). Kellert suggests that people and the activities they choose can be correlated with these values towards wildlife. Finally, consumptiveness of the activity (non-consumptive to consumptive) should be considered to illustrate that all forms of outdoor recreation and tourism have some type of impact-however insignificant—on the resource base, with some being less severe than others (consumptive forms of tourism include those that are said to consumer resources, such as hunting and fishing).

Despite how the term *nature tourism* has evolved in the recent past, it is still difficult to equate it with activities that are more consumptive in their orientation (e.g. hunting). The activities that we now group under nature tourism, including adventure tourism, fishing, hunting, whale watching, and ecotourism, might best be labelled *natural resource-based tourism*. This latter categorisation implies a element of use, which we know corresponds to any form of tourism that occurs outside and which relies specifically on the natural resource base. Furthermore, it is more analogous to the continuum of conservation (saving for use) and preservation (saving form use). Ecotourism, although it entails use, should apply more to the preservation end of this continuum, while hunting and fishing relate more to the aspect of conservation. This sentiment related to the work of Ewert (1997), who writes that 'resource-based' tourism includes a variety of tourism endeavours including ecotourism, adventure tourism, and indigenous tourism, and their various activities.

Nature Tourism in the USA

The recreation Executive report of the US Forest Service (1994) illustrates that nature-based recreation trends as we approach the year 2000 show increases in many non-consumptive outdoor activities. Outdoor photography is up 23 per cent, wildlife watching is up 16 per cent, backpacking is up 34 per cent, and day hiking is up 34 per cent. Also, the National Survey on Recreation and the Environment, a study conducted by the U.S. federal government, concluded that of a number of outdoor recreation activities, birding, hiking, and backpacking experienced the most significant growth in participation between 1982-83 and 1994-95. Birdwatching increased 155 per cent, hiking increased 93 per cent, and backpacking increased 73 per cent. Conversely, hunting and fishing experienced negative growth over his period of time (-12 per cent and –9 per cent, respectively). Further to this, the White House Conference on Tourism in October 1995 indicated the following with respect to the non-consumptive use of birds:

Number of participants:	$2.5 million
Retail sales:	$5 billion

Wages and Salaries:	$4 billion
Full and part-time jobs:	1,91,000
Tax revenues	
State sales:	$306 million
State income:	$74 million
Federal income:	$516 million
Total economic out put:	$16 billion

Adventure Tourism or Ecotourism?

A few hours of mountain climbing turn a villain and a saint into two rather equal creatures. Exhaustion is the shortest way to equality and fraternity-and liberty is added eventually by sleep.-Nietzsche.

A close cousin that has developed alongside ecotourism is adventure travel, which is some circles is felt to subsume ecotourism. For example, in suggesting that ecotourism is a branch of adventure tourism, Dyess (1997: 2) admits that he did not have a full appreciation of the heated disagreement that 'exists over the semantics of the two terms, as proponents of ecotourism and adventure travel strive to define and sanctify their own approach to travel'. In a general sense, differentiation between the two forms of travel can simply be based on the type of activity pursued (again, with respect to the primary motivation in participating in the activity). However, in cases where activities are broadly categorised as either ecotourism or adventure tourism, there may be problems, as evident in the following example. Tourism Canada has defined adventure tourism as 'an outdoor leisure activity that takes place in an unusual, exotic, remote or wilderness destination, involves some form of unconventional means of transportation, and tends to be associated with low or high levels of activity' (Canadian Tourism Commission 1995: 5). The following is a list of adventure travel activities developed by the Canadian Tourism Commission (CTC) under this definition:

(1) Nature Observation;

(2) Wildlife Viewing (e.g. birding, whale- watching);

(3) Water Adventure Products (e.g. canoeing, kayaking);

(4) Land Adventure Products (e.g. hiking, climbing);

(5) Winter Adventure Products (e.g. dog sledding, cross-country skiing); and

(6) Air Adventure Products, including hot air ballooning, hang-gliding, air safaris, bungee jumping, and parachuting.

The point to the made from this example Is that both ecotoruism and adventure tourism products may adhere to the CTC's definition, despite the fact that to many there is a clear distinction between nature observation (ecotourism) and kayaking (adventure tourism). Clearly, further analysis of these activities is required in order to detect similarities and differences. However, while activity is important (an outdoor pursuit) to identifying adventure activities. Priest (1990) writes that there must be an element of uncertainty associated with the event.

The answer to the question of how adventure and non-adventure tourism experiences like ecotourism differ may lie in the realm of social psychology, which examines why participation occurs from a cognitive and behavioural standpoint (instead of some arbitrary basis established on the basis of setting and other such variables) Both Ewert (1985) and Hall (1992) write that it is risk that plays a primary role in the decision to engage in adventurous activities. In addition, Hall suggests that it is the activity more than the setting that provides the dominant attraction for pursuit of adventure creation and tourism. Two other factors in analysing one's motivation to engage in risk-related activities include challenge and skill, the fundamental variables behind Csikszentmihaly's (1990) model of flow (see also Csikszentmihalyi and Csikzentmihalyi (1990). Individuals who are said to have reached a state of flow have matched their personal skills with the challenges of a particular activity. Flow includes a number of main elements as defined by Czikszentmihalyi. These include:

1. *Total immersion into the activity.* This relates to the elimination of distractions that enable the person to lose touch with his or her surroundings.

2. *Enhanced concentration.* A result of the previous factor that allows that participant to forget about the unpleasant tasks that may be associated with the activity.

3. *Actions directed at fulfilling the goal.* The goals and objectives of the event are clearly understood by the participant, who knows how best to approach the situation.

4. *The activity requires skills and challenge.* The relationship between these two variables is important in that if skill far exceeds challenge, boredom will result, whereas if challenge far exceeds skill, anxiety will result.

5. *Flow involves control.* The participant exercises control over his or her movements and the situation, with a degree of anticipation of the events which will unfold.

6. *A sense of transcendentaism.* Here the participant has the experience of transcending his or her physical being, as rooted on the face of the earth, to reach some higher level of understanding or being. A sense of oneness with the surroundings or objects involved in the experience is felt.

7. *The loss of time.* Frequently participants feel as though they have been involved for a short period of time (e.g. one hour), when in fact they have been involved for a long periods of time (e.g. for hours).

Czikszentmihalyi (1990) suggests that flow is not necessarily restricted to those who engage in adventurous activities, but also includes those, for example, playing chess of physicians engaged in surgery. According to Hall, then, it may be the desire or the enhanced desire to experience the state of flow that moves individuals to participate in risk or adventure-related activities.

The Quinn (1990), adventure lies deep within the spiritual, emotional, intellectual, and objective spheres of humanity; and is the external seduction of the hidden (Dufrene 1973; 398). More specifically, Quinn argues that adventure is a desire for a condition that is absent within the individual. Under rather tenuous conditions, the individual must harbour doubt as to the adequacy of his or her ability. The further one attempts to go beyond one's perceived personal talents, the more intense the adventurous situation becomes. It is this element of unknown that led Einstein to suggest that 'the most beautiful and deepest experience a man can have is the sense of the mysterious' (cited in Mayur 1996). The adventure experience therefore is one that is not discrete but rather one that varies in intensity. The result is that in today's marketplace, tourists are able to select for a broad range of hard and soft adventure experiences, offering associated degrees of risk and uncertainty. According to Christiansen (1990), it is the task of the adventure tour operator to provide the client with an adequate perception or risk, while ensuring a high level of safety and security. This is accomplished through an accident-free history, good-planning, and the maintenance of the highest level of leadership, skills, and experience. Christiansen provides a good understanding of the difference between soft-and hard-core adventure experiences. The soft adventure activities in the figure are pursued by those interested in a perceived risk and adventure with little actual risk, whereas the hard adventure examples included are known by both the participant and the serve provider to have a high level of risk (if, indeed a service provider is involved in the experience).

In related research the link between motivation and level of experience in mountain climbers was analysed by Ewert (1985), who based his research on the premise that the perception of danger is important in the experience of the risk recreation participant. From a survey of climbers at Mount Ranier National Park, Washington, he found that inexperienced climbers participated for recognition, escape, and social reasons. Conversely, the experienced climbers were motivated by more intrinsic reasons including exhilaration, challenge, personal testing, decision-making, and locus of control. The implications of the research are such that over time, climbers who continue with a risk recreation activity such as scuba-dividing, mountain climbing and spelunking (cave exploration) may require conditions that are less crowded, more rugged, and less controlled than their novice counterparts.

Fennell and Eagles (1990) focused on the element of risk in examining potential differences between adventure travel, ecotourism, and mass tourism in the framework. Here it is implied that preparation and training, known/ unknown results and risks, and certainty and safety are all variables that may be used to differentiate between these forms of tourism. The figure demonstrates that the three kinds of activity are not mutually exclusive; ecotourism may share some elements of the other two experiences, while still remaining distinct from mass tourism and adventure tourism.

Identifies the evolving relationship between three common AT products, namely ecotourism, adventure tourism and cultural tourism. As suggested earlier, the overlap between these three appears to have become stronger over the past few years, to the point where many studies, usually government or marketing ones (see CTC 1995 and Wight 1992), have considered them as almost completely synonymous (this phenomenon is represented by the acronym ACE in the figure). Depending on the setting and situation, ACE either expands or contracts to represent different concentrations of adventure, culture, and ecotourism, either in name alone or in product content. Those situations that are classed solely as ecotourism avoid the inclusion of conditions that relate to culture tourism or adventure tourism (or both). At the same time, there is the recognition that a continuum exists between hard-and soft-path ecotourism experiences (see Laarman and Durst 1987; Orams 1995). This figure (and the book) attempts to demonstrate that ecotourism should be considered as unique according to its function and role within the tourism marketplace, a stance which is based on the facts that (1) there is little empirical evidence demonstrating homogeneity between adventure tourism, culture tourism, and ecotourism, and (2) there may be an associated dilution factor or effect on ecotourism if these three types of tourism merge into a combined form.

Tourist Typologies

Perhaps as a function of the tremendous demand for different types of travel experiences tourism has blossomed with a rich array of terms describing different types of vacation experiences in different settings, with virtually no research available to describe these various 'types' systematically (Boyd 1991 identifies some 90 types of tourism). Historically, tourism research has tended to concentrate not on tourism types, but rather on tourist types and the various individual traits, characteristics, motivations, needs, and so on of travellers. This has ultimately enabled both researchers and practitioners to better understand tourists on the basis of the types of experiences they seek, as individuals and groups. The following section briefly examines a number of pertinent motivational/behavioural and social/cultural typologies, as a basis for understanding ecotourists.

Christaller quite effectively grosped the notion that, over time, a destination will play host to a rich variety of different types of travellers.

While tourist destinations were seen to be transformed under the influence of tourism, so did the type of traveller, either as a result of these changes or as responsible for initiating the changes within the region. Cohen (1972: 172) commented, echoing Chritaller, that 'Attractions and facilities which were previously frequented by the local population are gradually abandoned. As Greenwich Village became a tourist attraction, many of the original bohemians moved the east Village.' Cohen used this as an analogy to demonstrate that travellers were inherently different on the basis of their relationship to both the tourist business establishment and host country Accordingly, he grouped tourists into four categories, including organised mass tourists, individual mass tourists, explorers, and drifters. This typology reflected a continuum such that the organised mass tourist is seen as the least adventuresome with little motivation to leave the confines of his or her home environmental bubble. The drifter, in contrast, shunned the tourist establishment, searching for the most authentic travel experiences available.

Motivation, or the drive to satisfy inner physiological and psychological needs, has been fundamental to tourism researchers interested in the 'why' of tourist travel. To Pearce (1982), there needs to exist a stronger emphasis in linking role and motivations with social and environmental preferences of tourists, in order that destinations could be better matched with markets, travel expectations, and accommodation. Iso-Ahola (1982) suggested that travel motivation is purely psychological and not sociological in nature. He argued that people travel for basically two reasons: (1) to seek intrinsic rewards (novelty), and (2) to escape their everyday environments (escape). These two motivations may be either of a personal natural (personal troubles or failures) or interpersonal (related to co-workers, family, or neighbours). The amalgam of these elements is a four-cell matrix, where a single tourists could theoretically go through one or all aspects during the course of one trip.

MacCannell (1989) also considered the fundamental differences between traveller types in examining the social structure of tourist space based on 'front' and 'back' regions. Front regions are those readily experienced by tourists and places where hosts and guests regularly interact. Conversely, back regions are the preserve of the host and are essentially non-tourism oriented in their function. Tourists in search of authenticity penetrate back regions in the hope of acquiring real day-to-day mannerisms of residents. To what degree tourists are willing or able to penetrate back regions—in identified access zones of tourism areas—may be important to their achieving their overall purpose. Although these 'places' are actual locations in the conventional economic/ geographical context, in the mind of the tourist or tourist group they hold special value in defining the travel experience. In general, these back regions are sociological.

Profiling the Ecotourist

Some of the earliest studies on ecotourism attempted to classify ecotoutists on the basis of setting, experience, and group dynamics.

For example, Kusler (1991) typified ecotourists as belonging to three main groups, including:

1. *Do-it-yourself ecotoursts*. Despite their relative amonymity, this group comprise the largest percentage of all ecotourists. These individuals stay in a variety of different types of accommodations, and have the

mobility to visit any number of settings. Their experience, therefore, is marked by a high degree of flexibility.

2. *Ecotourists on tours.* This group expects a high degree of organisation within their tour, and travel to exotic destinations (e.g. Antartica).

3. *School groups or scientific groups.* This group often become involved in scientific research of an organisation or individual, often stay in the same region for extensive periods of time, and are willing to endure harsher size conditions than other ecotourists.

Conversely, Lindberg (1991:3) emphasises the importance of dedication and time as a function of defining different types of ecotoruists, including what tourists wish to experience from ecotourism, where they wish to travel, and how they wish to travel, Lindberg identified four basic types:

1. *Hard-core nature tourists:* Scientific researchers or members of tours specifically designed for education, removal of litter, or similar purposes;

2. *Dedicated nature tourists*: People who take trips specifically to see protected areas and who want to understand local natural and cultural history;

3. *Mainstream nature tourists*: People who visit the Amazon, the Rwandan gorilla park, or other destinations primarily to take an unusual trip; and

4. *Casual nature tourists*: People who experience nature incidentally as part of a broader trip.

Consistent with the increase in ecotourism opportunities, and the associated typologies of tourists travelling on such trips, has been an increase in the volume of literature available on the ecotourism, with much of it focusing on presenting a profile of this type. Initial studies decidedly pointed to the fact that the ecotourist was predominantly male, well educated wealthy, and long-staying. For example, Wilson (1987: 21) reported the following in researching 62 tourists visiting Ecuador:

> The male/female ratio was 52% to 48%, and the mean average age was 42... Twenty-seven percent earned a family income between US $30,000 to $60,000, before taxes annually. Approximately one-quarter earned more than $90,000 per year. About 30% had bachelors degrees, and a little over 10% had doctoral degrees.

Both Fennell and Smale (1992) and Reingold (1993) report similar results in their work on Canadian ecotourists. On average, the Canadian ecotourists in the Fennel and Smale study were 54 years of age, with the majority in the 60-69 age cohort. The sample was predominantly male (55 per cent), earned on average about CDN$60,000, with almost one-third and two-thirds having undergraduate and graduate degrees, respectively. According to these authors, this education is well above the national average of about 19 per cent and 4 per cent of Canadians having a bachelor's degree and graduate training, respectively. In Reingold's work, 24 per cent of Canadian ecotourists were 55 to 64 years of age, 36 per cent had annual incomes over $70,000, 65 per cent had a university degree; however, 64 per cent of the respondents of this study were female. This latter statistic goes against much of the previous research suggesting that males are slightly more representative of this group. The general outdoor recreation literature supports the fact that most participants—two-third or even three—quarters-are of the male gender (Hendee *et al.* 1990).

The studies involving ecotourists have been found to mirror related research on bird watchers. For example, Applegate and Clark (1987) report that more men than women birdwatch and that they have strikingly high levels of affluence and education. More than 50 per cent of the respondents of their study had completed four years of college and had annual family incomes in excess of US$20,000. The findings of Kellert (1985) indicate that committed birders were 73 per cent male with an average age of 42. Committed birders were also far better educated (nearly two-thirds had college and/or graduate school education) and had higher incomes than responents who did not birdwatch. As more studies of this nature surface in the future it will be interesting to see how the profile of the ecotourists changes (or stays the same) as a function of many variables, including the types of experiences and products offered to ecotourists, and the maturity of the industry.

Beyond an analysis of socio-demographics, Fennell and Smale (1992) directly compared the average Canadian tourist against a sample of ecotourists (based on the work of Fennell 1990). These researchers used the results of a 1983 Canadian study (Tourism Attitude and Motivation Study (CTAMS) that analysed the general attitudes and benefits sought by a sample of 11,501 Canadian tourists. The questions used in the CTAMS were study duplicated and applied to a sample of ecotourists who had recently returned form a Costa Rican ecoturism trip between 1988 and 1989. Of 98 surveys mailed to the ecotoruists (tourists were contacted by obtaining mailing lists of Canadian ecotour operators offering programmes in Costa Rica), 77 were returned and usable.

In general the findings illustrate that the benefits sought by ecotourists may be found in new, active, and adventuresome activities and involvements; while the Canadian population benefits were more strongly related to sedentary activity and family-related endeavours. Ecotourists were found to pursue attractions related to the outdoors (wilderness areas, parks and protected areas, and rural areas); while attractions related to cities and resorts were more important to the average Canadian traveller. The implications of the research are such that they empirically demonstrate that there is indeed a difference between ecotourists and general travellers in terms of their trip related needs and focus. Kretchman and Eagles (1990) and Willacy and Eagles (1990) followed the initial survey design of Fennell (1990) in comparing ecotourists in a variety of different settings. These studies were combined by Eagles (1992) in a comprehensive overview of the travel motivations of Canadian ecotourists. His results generally substantiate the results of Fennell and Smale (1992), above, in suggesting that ecotourists are fundamentally different, in their travel motivations, from the average traveller.

As suggested earlier, an effective way in which to differentiate between types of tourists visiting particular regions is through an examination of various personal characteristics such as primary motives, benefits sought, and so on. Turnbull (1981), however, provides an interesting argument against such an approach. He suggests that although on the surface nature tourists travelling to Africa state that it is primarily the animals that bring them to the game parks of East Africa, on the basis of his observations she feels that the reasons for visiting Africa run much deeper. As an anthropologist, Turnbull believes that perhaps latently it is also the 'Africa' and the 'Kilimanjaro' that bring such tourists to this setting. In essence, he believes that people want to tap into their distant past when humans had a much stronger relationship with animals, seeing them as something more than just prey to be hunted, and it is to experience something of this relationship that is really desired by present-day tourists. He states that the tourists.

This theory gives us another means by which to further examine the intergroup differences that exist between various forms of tourism (*i.e.* ecotourists and non-ecotourists), but also the intragroup differences (*i.e.* soft-path ecotourists and hard-path ecotourists) as well.

Table 1.1: Relative importance of selected attractions and benefits to Canadian travellers and ecotourisms[a]

Variable	*General Population*		*Canadian Ecotourists*	
	Mean[b]	*s.d.*	*Mean*	*s.d*
Benefits to ecotourists[c] Experiencing new and different life styles	2.67	1.02	1.95	0.78
Trying new foods	2.85	0.99	2.43	0.82
Being physically active	2.36	1.03	1.88	0.92
Visiting historical places	2.71	1.04	2.35	0.74
Seeing as much as possible	2.01	0.99	1.77	0.81
Being daring and adventuresome	2.91	0.98	2.62	1.01
Meeting people with similar interests	2.08	0.94	0.91	0.71
Population[c]watching sports	3.16	0.96	3.84	0.37
Visiting friends and relatives	1.83	1.03	3.25	0.82
Doing nothing at all	2.86	1.00	3.72	0.60
Being together as a family	1.66	0.98	2.92	1.04
Reliving past good times	2.46	1.06	3.36	0.79
Visiting places my family came from	2.70	1.16	3.45	0.84
Feeling at home away from home	1.81	0.91	2.64	0.93
Having fun and being entertained	1.95	0.88	2.72	0.94
Important attractions to ecotourists[c]				
Wilderness areas	2.34	1.09	1.06	0.37
National parks and reserves	2.21	1.01	1.14	0.35
Rural areas	2.34	0.94	1.49	0.60
Mountains	2.34	1.07	1.50	0.66
Lakes and streams	2.05	0.99	1.57	0.59
Historic sites and parks	2.37	1.01	2.05	0.81
Cultural activities	2.66	0.97	2.32	0.87
Oceanside	2.15	1.07	1.97	0.78
Attractions to population[c]Indoor sports	2.98	0.94	3.85	0.35
Amusement and theme parks	2.74	0.99	3.80	0.54
Nightlife and entertainment	2.72	1.04	3.70	0.56
Gambling	3.61	0.69	3.96	0.34
Shopping	2.45	1.01	3.14	0.74
Resort areas	2.56	1.01	3.26	0.82
Big cities	2.94	0.93	3.39	0.69
Beaches for swimming/sunning	2.34	1.10	2.79	0.96
Predictable weather	2.11	0.97	2.40	0.81
Live theatre and musicals	2.99	1.01	3.21	0.91

Source: Funnell and Smale 1992

Notes: (a) Differences between general population and ecotourists are statistically significant at 0.05 level.

(b) Scale : 1 = 'very important'; 4 = 'not at all important'

(c) Attractions/benefits are in descending rank order based on magnitude of difference between groups.

as is our understanding of how ecotourism differs from other types of tourism. More research is needed to help formulate definitions acceptable to those working in the field, to help overcome this critical absence of focus. The literature points to the fact that ecotourism is one aspect of nature-oriented tourism, which includes many other types of tourism and outdoor recreation, both consumptive and non-consumptive. Ecotourism is said to relate to adventure travel only inasmuch as it shares similar environmental settings. Differentiation between these two forms of tourism must be done on the basis of social psychology.

CHAPTER TWO

Evaluation and Monitoring of Ecotourism: Growth and Development

The last two decades has revealed a growing awareness that economic benefits alone can no longer be the only measure of success when assessing visitation to unique natural, cultural, and historical sities, and the surrounding communities. Recognising this paradox, demand for a sustainable conservation/tourism balance has grown. It is a tourism philosophy that considers the natural social, cultural, and economic issues equally in assessing the value and impact of tourism.

The response from the tourism industry has been a concept known as ecotourism. For a term that has only been seen in tourism and resource management literature primarily during the past decade, ecotourism has received considerable attention, with no drop off foreseen as we head into the 21st century. Its origination is a reaction to the perceived negative impacts caused by mass tourism to natural areas. As a result, the idea of ecotourism inevitably owes its conception to the developing interest of resource managers, tourism officials, and community leaders. In essence, it is a mechanism that can aid in the conservation of our natural, cultural, and historical resources while still providing the economic incentive to do so. Ecotourism is about creating and appeasing a hunger for nature, about utilising tourism's potential for conservation and economic development, and about deterring its negative impact on ecology, culture, and aesthetics (Western, 1993). Thenotion of visiting and experiencing unique and authentic natural areas while also protecting the integrity of them and the surrounding local communities has become in the 1990's, an acceptable and marketable mechanism for the tourism industry. Its placement in the turism industry as a nature-based form of specialty travel has been defined a number of ways during its relatively short history (Ceballos-Lascurain, 1991; Farrell & Runyan, 1991; Scace, Grifone, & Usher, 1992; TIES, 1993; Ziffer, 1989), with each providng a fairly similar conception. For purposes of this paper, ecotourism is defined as irresponsible travel to natural areas which conserves the environment and sustains the well-being of local people (TIES, 1993). Although no firm estimaties, due to definitional difficulties, have been made for ecotourists, Filion has estimated that of the 528.4 million international tourists in 1994, 40 to 60% were nature tourists, and 20 to 40% were wildlife-related tourists (Eco-Source, 1995).

In the United Staties alone, the U.S. Travel Data Centre estimated that some 43 million U.S. adults took a nature-based trip between 1992 and 1995 (Eco-Source, 1995). Ecotourism has been lauded as an attractive sustainable development alternative to mass tourism because it is perceived to have fewer negative impacts on natural resources while also providing incentive to adopt practices that conserve and potentially enhance the very resources it is so dependent on (Farrell & Runyan, 1991; Wight, 1993). As Wight (1995) suggests, truly sustainable ecotourism should involve education among all parties – local communities, government, non-governmental organizations, industry, and tourists before, during, and after the trip. Further, it should instill ethical responsibilities and behaviour towards the natural and cultural environment while promoting long-term benefits to all connected parties, be it economic, educational or life-supporting. Much of the ecotourism sector (*i.e.,* suppliers, tour operators, local communities) has positioned itself in the tourism industry to do just that – educate and instill ethical responsibility – and the so-called ecotourists have come to expect certain conservation-minded practices be in place at the various destinations visited worldwide.

Professional associations have been formed and codes of ecotourism ethics, standards, and guidelines produced to aid in the management of the ecotourism product (Orams, 1995). Overwhelmingly, the majority of these voluntary guidelines and standards encourage travellers, tour operators, and guides, to strengthen their efforts to support conservation in the ecotourism destinations. The National Audubon Society, The Ecotourism Association of Australia, Canadian Environmental Advisory Council, The International Ecotourism Society, are but a handful of organizations that have designed, in effect, a road map that provides interested parties with information needed to pursue these established objectives.

However, Goodale and Cater (1996) found that voluntary codes of conduct provide excellent guidance on objectives and principles, but are of little practical use to tourism businesses and destinations. The authors identified two underlying problems associated with ecotourism guidelines: (1) The production and implementation of guidelines are voluntary and lack legislative backing, and (2) guidelines are just one aspect of a needed comprehensive sustainable tourism strategy. According to Goodale and Cater, the limits of industry self-regulation results in gaps between the current level of performance by the tourism industry and the desired state of sustainable tourism. The three gaps described were:

(a) The tactical gap between the best and worst tourism business,

(b) the strategic gap between the environmental performance of the best tourism business and the performance level that could be achieved through applying best environmental business practices, and

(c) the absolute gap between the best environmental option and true sustainability.

Even with the voluntary guidelines available, inappropriate developments are taking place in attractive and sensitive locations. Without giving due regard to the underlying principles of ecotourism, private operators and even governmental agencies seem to be securing the short-term economic benefits to sell regions or products (Jarvie, 1991; Wight, 1993). The Ecotourism Society neatly summed up the problem by describing this sell perspective, warning customers of the dubious claim of eager travel marketers who exploit the trend towards integrating environmental values into vacation choices... the public at large must continue choosing from among destinations and tour operators who mostly package nirvana and paradise like nut bars and soap.

There is now growing concern among many of the organisations and associations who have introduced guidelines, as well as the local cultures and communities that are being impacted by ecotourism, that a better understanding of the ecotourism product needs to addressed. Butler (1990, p. 41) suggested that, to promote one form of tourism as a solution to the multiple problems which can be caused by extensive and long term tourism development is somewhat akin to selling nineteenth century wonder medicines. Making simplistic and idealized comparisons of mass and ecotourism, such that one is obviously undesirable and the other close to perfection is not only inappropriate, it is also deceiving (Butler, 1990, p. 41). Butler's point is that ecotourism is not always considerate, optimising, planned and under control. Sometimes it is quite the opposite and more akin to mass tourism when evaluated in terms of overall impact – social, environment, economic and cultural.

It is precisely because of the concerns as expressed above, that tourism officials, are suggesting that a transition needs to be made into certification and evaluation programmes that, at the very least, encourage companies to consider improving their practices (Cecil, 1995). The inevitable question is how long can we continue to promote ecotourism to our world's protected and unprotected natural areas if left unregulated or unchecked? Recently, the Australian Office of National Tourism working with the Ecotourism Association of Australia and the Australian Tourism Operators Association have jointly developed the National Ecotourism Accreditation Programme (NEAP) Ecotourism Association of Australia, 1996). This voluntary programme is designed to provide industry and consumers with an assurance that an accredited ecotourism product or service is backed by a commitment to best practice environmental management and the provision of quality ecotourism experiences. The NEAP has been developed for ecotourism businesses and protected area agencies offering accommodations, tours, or attractions who comply with eight principles of ecotourism. The accreditation process consists of a combination of self-assessment, an external review by an appointed administrator, and final review by an accreditation panel. To check on the reliability of the applicants, verification via feedback from clients, feedback from referees, and audits of ecotourism businesses.

Evaluation and Monitoring

As this segment of the global travel industry grows, there has emerged proposals for objective criteria to evaluate ecotourism suppliers and destinations, and to monitor the level of conservation affiliation and the extent of their impacts (Hiller, 1991; Holland, 1992; Shores, 1992). Hawkins, (Cecil, 1995, p. 16) summed up the situation by suggesting, people are looking for more than just words...they are looking for concrete actions and practices. While not all ecotourists may be looking for specific concrete actions and practices, there are many who travel with high expectations related to the natural environment and who have come to expect certain sustainable practices be in place (Kretchman & Eagles, 1990; Eagles 1992). In their evaluation of registered ecotour lodges in Amazonas, Brazil, Wallace and Pierce (1996) found that ecotour ventures only partially satisfied the ecotourism principles that were used. Specifically, the authors found that ecotourism provided employment, improved access, new services (*i.e.,* health utilities), and made some local purchases. However, their research found that ecotours did not contribute greatly to conservation education, resource protection, and the involvement or empowerment of the indigenous population.

There is a growing number of organisations who believe it is time to objectively evaluate ecotourism suppliers and destinations. There is indeed, developing interest in the travel and tourism industry to offer some type of a stamp of approval (*i.e.,* Good Housekeeping Seal of Approval) to those suppliers and destinations who meet certain standards that reflect environmental and social responsibility for the particular sectors of the tourism industry they represent. Examples of such programmes include: Green Globe (created by the World Travel & Tourism Council), Green Leaf (by the Pacific Asia Travel Association), and Green Evaluation (by The Ecotourism Society). It is believed by those involved in these innovative evaluation and monitoring programmes that designations like these can provide travel agents and the ecotourist with the kind of information needed in evaluating the level of environmental and social responsibility practiced by participating travel suppliers and destinations (Cecil, 1995). Although it may be a while before any of these designations carry the equivalence of the Good Housekeeping Seal of Approval, many industry leaders feel this is a step in the right direction if many concerned ecotourists have their say.

Green Evaluations Project

Of the organizations sponsoring ecotourism certification for suppliers and destinations, the International Ecotourism Society's Green Evaluation programme may hold promises. Unlike many of the others which mostly rely on sources inside the sponsoring organisation to evaluate participants practices and adherence to principles, TIES is relying on an independent evaluation of participating nature-based tour operators through the use of consumer surveys and the analysis of such by a neutral party (*e.g.*, academic institution) for adherence information. It is generally recognized that programme sponsors and funding sources can rarely act completely independently or autonomously. As a result, TIES believes independent evaluation of participating tour operators by a neutral source should be mandatory if an ecotourism certification programme is to have any real credibility. To do otherwise, taints the objectivity of the programmes at the root (Cecil, 1995, p. 17).

TIES Ecotourism Guidelines for Nature Tour Operators

- Prepare travellers to minimise their negative impacts while visiting sensitive environments and cultures before departure.
- Prepare travellers for each encounter with local cultures

and with native animals and plants.

- Minimise visitor impacts on the environment by offering literature, briefings, leading by example, and taking corrective actions.
- Minimise traveler impacts on local cultures by offering literature, briefings, leading by example and taking corrective actions.
- Use adequate leadership and maintain small enough to ensure minimum group impact on destinations. Avoid areas that are undermanaged and overvisited.
- Ensure managers, staff and contract employees know and participate in all aspects of company policy to prevent impacts on the environment and local cultures.
- Give managers, staff and contract employees access to programmes that will upgrade their ability to communicate with and manage clients in sensitive natural and cultural settings.
- Be a contributor to the conservation of the regions being visited.
- Provide competitive, local employment in all aspects of business operations.
- Offer site-sensitive accommodations that are not wasteful of local resources or destructive to the environment that provide ample opportunity for learning about the environment and sensitive interchange with local communities.

In 1993, TIES took several important steps to establish standards of performance for the nature-based tourism industry. One of those steps was the formulation and publication of Ecotourism Guidelines for Nature Tour Operators. Drafted by a group of conservationists, tour operators, and academics, responding to the growing nature of ecotourism and the discussion and debate about a need for ethical standards to guide the growth, the guidelines are an attempt to bring to the forefront what the state of the art of delivering ecotourism services should be in the 1990's. The document not only provided guidelines on what should be observed by nature tour operators, but also how these services should be delivered, with what objectives, and for whose benefit. It is suggested that ecotourism businesses, conservation organisations, governments, developers, hotels properties, the press and consumers could benefit from the evaluation process.

While it is recognized that monitoring and evaluation programmes in the field of ecotourism are still in their infancy, and funding to support them is not readily available on any scale, it is hoped that TIES's Green Evaluations Project may become a prototype for future monitoring programmes. The underlying goal being that by factoring a monitoring programme into the development of ecotourism projects both large and small scale, the ability to predict its success in meeting the needs of interested parties (*i.e.*, corporations, governments, consumers, and conservation organisations), may result in a long-term sustainable product. The primary purpose of this project was to develop and tiest a consumer evaluation programme for nature tour operators based upon TIES guidelines. The specific objectives of this project were to:

1. To develop a process which evaluates the performance of nature tour operators using TIES's Ecotourism Guidelines for Nature Tour Operators in Ecuador.
2. To provide information which will enable TIES to market ecotourism Guidelines for Nature Tour Operators.
3. To implement the consumer evaluation programme in Ecuador during a 17 month study period starting in April of 1995.

Based on the project's established research objectives, three study outcomes were identified. The anticipated outcomes of this project were:

1. To use this process as a method to understand how well Ecuadorean nature tour operators are complying with and implementing TIES's guidelines.
2. To understand whether the means used to evaluate nature tour operators is reasonable, fair, and has merit as a tool to certify or rate nature tour operators in Ecuador and elsewhere.
3. To evaluate this prototype monitoring programme for its potential in helping to predict the success of sustainable ecotourism development, both large and small scale, worldwide.

Research Methods

The Recreation, Travel & Tourism Institute (RTTI) at Clemson University, USA, was contracted to design, develop and analyze a tool and method which could be used to measure compliance with TIES's, Ecotourism Guidelines for Nature Tour Operators. By contracting with a third party, TIES hoped to eliminate potential bias inherent in self-evaluation by nature tour operators (Rossi & Freeman, 1993). The resulting 8-page questionnaire was designed in such a manner that travelers could complete it within approximately ten minutes. It consisted of the following six sections with the respective number of questions per section listed in parentheses: Pre-Departure Information (4) Visitor Information and Education Provided During the Trip (3), Tour Operator Contributions to Conservation and Local Development Programmes (5), Tour Operator Impact Management Programme (5), Evaluation of Local Accommodations (2), and Socio-Demographic Information About Ecotourist (14). The questionnaire was designed in such a way that nine of the ten guidelines proffered by TIES could be evaluated by the consumer. The lone guideline that was not addressed was, giving managers, staff and contract employees access to programmes that will upgrade their ability to communicate with and manage clients in sensitive natural and cultural settings. This guideline, although implied and probably reflected through the service provided by the tour operator, was beyond the range of consumer evaluation.

The site chosen for the pilot study was the country of Ecuador, because of its unofficially endorsed governmental support and interest in ecotourism as well as its willingness to participate in this pilot project. TIES worked in conjunction with the Ecuadorean Ecotourism Association (EEA), housed in Ecuador, and it was through their efforts that a Spanish version of Ecotourism Guidelines for Nature Tour Operators was made available in early 1994, to all Ecuadorean nature tour operators who were interested in receiving them. In August 1994, three general orientation meetings regarding the proposed Green Evaluations Project were held in the Ecuadorean cities of Quito, Guayaquil, and Cuenca. All Ecuadorean nature tour operators were invited to attend. Upon completion of the orientation meetings, 32 Ecuadorean nature tour operators, responsible for approximately 65% of the Ecuadorean ecotourism visitors, were identified that were willing to participate in this proposed project. The 32 participating nature tour operators, ranging in size from serving one to nearly forty thousand clients yearly, then had just over six months to implement the TIES guidelines and to make the necessary changes in their business operations.

The administration of the survey began on April 1, 1995 and ended on August 31, 1996. In March 1995, a total of 4,010 survey instruments, in four languages (i.e., English, Spanish, German, and French), were forwarded to EEA for distribution to 32 participating nature tour operators (Note: An additional nature tour operator was added to the study after the original thirty-one had been identified). Each tour operator was to be given enough questionnaires to randomly sample 10% of their yearly clients and were to administer the questionnaires across all 17 months of the project in a equitable manner that reflected their business cycles. For instance, if the operator had some very busy months with a high number of ecotourists, then a proportionate number of questionnaires should be administered during those months to reflect the increased ecotourists. Further, if they had too few ecotourists one month then they were to select additional ecotourists the next month to achieve the desired overall number.

Nature tour operators were required to administer the questionnaires to their clients at the beginning of the tour with the instructions that ecotourists were to respond to the questionnaires as the respective tours progressed. All completed questionnaires were to be sealed in an envelope by the ecotourists collected by their respective tour operator, and returned to EEA. The Ecuadorean Ecotourism Association, in turn, mailed the completed questionnaires to Clemson University for analysis. Another method in which Clemson University received completed questionnaires was when the ecotourist took the survey instrument home with them for completion and returned them via personal mail. This represented approximately 10% of the total received. At the end of the 17 month study period, a total of 608 completed questionnaires had been received for analysis. Of the original 4,010 survey instruments that were to be distributed to the 32 tour operators, 373 were removed from the analysis due to four tour operators either going out of business or dropping out of the study. An additional 459 survey instruments were removed due to five tour operators failure to actually participate in the administration of the questionnaires. Furthermore, an additional 732 were returned by participating operators as unadministered. As a result, the total number of useable survey instruments for analysis was 2,446. Therefore, the overall survey response rate was approximately twenty-five percent (24.9%). Of the 608 completed questionnaires, 415 were written in English, 128 in German, 29 in Spanish and 36 in French.

Study Limitations

In examining the process of evaluating and monitoring nature tour operators a number of issues have become readily apparent in measuring compliance with TIES guidelines. While the majority of nature tour operators were very supportive of the Green Evaluations process, a number of survey administration and collection problems were encountered. Out of the original 4,010 questionnaires that were to be distributed to the 32 participating nature tour operators for the study period (April 1, 1995 through August 31, 1996), a total of 608 completed or partially completed survey instruments were returned to Clemson University. This problem is manifested in that researchers will only be able to statistically evaluate with any validity compliance with TIES guidelines for seven of the participating nature tour operators. Of the original 32 nature tour operators participating in the project, 23 returned completed or partially completed questionnaires for analysis. Of which, nine of the 23 operators accounted for 82.6% of the total questionnaires received by Clemson University. Lastly, four nature tour operators either went out of business or dropped out during the study period, with an additional five choosing not to administer any questionnaires.

Socio-demographic Information

In an effort to develop a profile of the Ecuadorean ecotourists, a series of questions were developed on sociodemographic characteristics of the survey respondents. Respondents had a median age of 50 years, were 56.4% women, 68.9% had at least a college degrees, and 48.3% have a combined yearly income of $80,000 or greater. Over one-third (36.9%) had a Master's Degree or more. One-half (53.7%) of the respondents were from the United States, 38.9% were from Europe, and 3.0% were from South America.

These results are similar to findings by Kretchman and Eagles (1990), Williacy & Eagles (1990), Fennell (1990) and Ballantine (1991).

Trip Characteristics

Two-thirds of the ecotourists did not consider any other destination before deciding to travel to Ecuador and 83.2% were first-time visitors. The median amount of total expected expenses for the entire trip was $4,500 with 33.4% spending over $5,000. Finally, nearly 71% of the respondents were travelling as part of a packaged tour with 49.2% booking their tour in the United States, 35.3% in a country other than the US and 15.5% in Ecuador.

Pre-Departure Information

It is generally recognised that receiving trip related information prior to departure helps to strengthen and/or dispel certain travel expectations. Not only can effective pre-departure ecotourism literature provide this, but it can also act as a mechanism for environmental education which is customarily considered part of an ecotourism package. Nearly eighty-eight percent (87.7%) of the individuals who responded to the question (n=490), received pre-departure information about their tour prior to departure. Of which 96.9% actually read the information (n=475). For those that

The Number of Completed Questionnaires Received from the 32 Original Participating Nature Tour Operators

Nature Tour Operator	*# Received*
Adria Travel	0
Angermeyer Enchanted Exped.	33
Cabanas Alinahui	7

Canodros	81
Chasquitur	18
Ecoventura Tours	77
Ecuadorean Tours Quito	5
EcuadoreanTours Guayaquil	0
Entnotur	4
Etica	0
Expediciones Apullacta	3
Expediciones Dayuma	20
Explorandes	0
Galasam	0
Klein Tours	50
Latitud Cero	0
Magic Ecuador	0
Metropolitan Touring	13
Native Life	12
Netropic Turis	1
Nuevo Mundo	113
Pamir Travels	0
Quasar Nautica	41
Rolf Wittmer Tourism	43
Samoa Turismo	15
Sangay Touring	4
Supernova	0
Transturi	23
Tropic Ecologic Tours	8
Turismundial	4
Viajes Orion	12
Wilderness Travel	21
Total	608

Table 2.1: Sociodemographic Characteristics of Respondents

Gender	*Frequency*	*Percentage*
Female	323	56.4
Male	250	43.6
EDUCATION		
High school diploma or less	77	14.0
College degree, some college or technical/trade school	212	38.6
Graduate degree or some grade school	261	47.4
GROSS FAMILY INCOME IN $US		
Under $20,000	32	8.2
$20,000 to $39,999	64	16.4
$40,000 to $59,999	75	19.2
$60,000 to $79,999	31	7.9
$80,000 to $110,000	67	17.1
Over $110,000	122	31.2
AGE		
14 to 29	83	14.9
30 to 39	86	15.5
40 to 49	107	19.2
50 to 59	135	24.3
60 to 69	110	19.8
70 and above	35	6.3
CITIZENSHIP		
North America	308	53.7

Europe	223	38.9
South America	17	3.0
Other	26	4.1

Table 2.2: Trip Characteristics of Respondents

	Frequency	*Percentage*
Did you consider other ecotourism destinations before deciding to travel to Ecuador?		
Yes	186	33.9
No	363	66.1
Did you travel to Ecuador for any other purpose than ecotourism?		
Yes	115	20.6
No	442	79.4
Including this trip, how many times have you visited Ecuador?		
One	457	83.2
Two	45	8.2
Three	14	2.6
Expected expenses for this entire trip?		
$3,000 or less	106	22.2
$3,001 to $5,000	204	43.8
$5,001 to $7,000	71	15.2
$7,001 to $9,000	36	7.7
$9,001 or more	49	10.5
Part of a packaged tour?		
Yes	394	70.9
No	162	29.1
Composition of travel party*		
Spouse	220	38.2
Friends and/or professional colleagues	169	29.3

Tour group	149	26.0
Additional family members	116	20.2
Other	91	16.1
Alone	79	13.7

* Totals more than 100% due to multiple responses

received and read the pre-departure information, warnings against bringing disposable goods (15.8%) received the smallest amount of attention from the nature tour operators according to the respondents. Information on how to avoid accidental transport of alien species of plants and animals (33.3%) also received a nominal amount of attention according to the respondents.

Visitor Information and Education Provided during the Trip

Wight (1995) suggests, sustainable ecotourism should involve education among all parties before, during, and after the trip. Table 14.4 depicts the proportion of respondents who felt they were prepared via briefings, literature, and examples to enhance their understanding of the fragility of the area, how to avoid adverse environmental impacts and minimise their impact on local cultures.

As can be seen, there was fairly strong support that tour operators were providing information and education regarding the fragility of natural environment during the respective nature tours. Nearly nine out of ten (87.2%) of the respondents reported that they were briefed prior to each stop of their tour, with 82.9% reporting that briefings on proper behaviour while on trails, in comp sites, around wildlife or fragile plants, took place. The two areas of mild concern are the advisement against purchasing specific craft that are produced from threatened natural resources (69.4%) and the discouragement of having unrealistic expectations of observing rare wildlife or plants (60.7%). Overall, there is not as strong support for the provision of information to minimise cultural impacts as was provided by the tour operators in an effort to minimise environmental impacts. While 83.4% of the respondents felt that information was provided about local natural history, only 29.7% felt they were prepared as to how to respond to begging, with just 48.6% understanding whether it is acceptable to bargain for goods and how to do it.

Tour Operator Contributions to Conservation and Local Development Programmes

Another area considered fundamental to the sustainability of ecotourism is nature tour operator contributions to conservation and local development programmes. Table 14.5 represents the percentage of respondents who observed if their tour operator was contributing to profit and/or non-profit conservation and development programmes in Ecuador, was facilitating visitor contributions, and did encourage visitors to write government and/or corporate organisations in Ecuador whose policies were damaging. Over sixty percent (62.8%) of the respondents reported that their tour operator was contributing to profit and/ or non-profit conservation and development programmes. Although, this percentage could potentially be higher due to the 23.2% who were

Table 2.3: Visitor Information and Education Provided During the Trip

	Frequency	*Percentage**
A general orientation or overview at the beginning of your tour	518	89.5
Briefings prior to each stop of your tour	504	87.2
Informaton about local natural history	482	83.4
Briefings on proper behaviour on trails, in campsites, etc.	480	82.9
Advisement against collecting souvenirs from natural areas	479	82.6

Informative discussions to and from destinations and/or sities	463	80.0
Informationon local regulations with which you must comply	443	76.6
Information about the level of physical difficulty	441	76.3
Advisement on how to avoid adverse impacts of your visit in natural areas	431	74.2.
Advisement against purchasing products made from threatened flora/fauna	403	69.4
Briefings on proper behaviour with trash, human waste, fires, etc	386	66.9
Information on history of local cultures	377	65.2
Advisement against unrealistic expectations of observing rare flora/fauna	352	60.7
Acceptable behaviour when photographing local culture/people	343	59.3
When to pay gratuity, how much to pay, and to whom	336	58.3
Information about local cultural values	318	55.2
If it is acceptable to bargain for goods being purchased	280	48.6
How to respond to any begging which may be encountered	170	29.7

* Equals the percentage of respondents who replied yes for each query listed.

uncertain (N/A), also reveals a much higher number of respondents uncertain (N/A) as to whether their tour operator was providing contributions to strictly local non-profit conservation initiatives (65.4%), with 34.3% of the respondents unsure whether their tour operator was facilitating visitor contributions during the trip, and 34.8% unsure whether their tour operator encouraged respondents to write to government and/or corporate organisations whose policies were damaging to the environment and/or local cultures.

Table 2.4: Tour Operator Contributions to Conservation and Local Development Programmes in Ecuador

	Yes (%)	*No (%)*	*N/A (%)*
Observed that your tour operator is making contributions in Ecuador (n=551)	62.8	14.0	23.2
Facilitates visitor contributions to local conservation initiatives during the trip (n=551)	43.2	22.5	34.3
Provides corporate contributions to local non-profit conservation initiatives (n=538)	26.0	8.6	65.4
Encouraged you to write to government and/or corporate organisations whose policies are damaging to the environment and/oı local cultures (n=546)	25.8	39.2	34.8

Finally, respondents were asked to observe if tour operators have integrated locally owned businesses into aspects of their nature tour operations. It appears that the tour operators are generally contributing to the local economies visited via the hiring and purchasing practices observed by the respondents. It also appears that tour operators are doing a relatively good job in involving individuals, entrepreneurs and businesses into their operations. This was especially true for transportation services (83.2%). Over one-half of the respondents indicated that their tour operators secured locally owned services from restaurants (70.7%), local guides (58.6%) and food and craft vendors (56.1%), local guides (58.6%) and food and craft vendors (56.1%). Unfortunately, a relatively large percentage were unable to determine whether or not locally owned businesses and services were being utilised.

Table 2.5: Local Involvement in Tour Operators Business Functions Did tour operator hire or purchase services from locally owned businesses

	Yes (%)	*No (%)*	*N/A (%)*
Transportation (*e.g.*, vehicles, boats, etc.) (n=566)	83.2	6.0	10.8
Restaurants (n=546)	70.7	13.4	15.9
Guides from each community being visited (n=553)	58.6	21.0	20.4
Food and craft vendors (n=538)	56.1	15.6	28.3

Tour Opertor Impact Management Programme

Ecotourists were asked to evaluate how well the nature tour operators addressed impacts on the environment and local culture. Nearly all (96.2%) of the respondents felt the tour operators provided enough guides to manage the tour group. Respondents were then asked to report how often (*i.e.*, never, rarely, sometime, frequently, always) their tour guides communicated, encouraged or explained how to prevent impacts on the environment and local cultures. As can be seen in Table 2.6, it appears that tour guides did a very good job of communicating to the ecotourists important concerns regarding impacts on the environment and the local cultures by visitors to these special areas. In seven out of eight questions, nearly 80% of the tour guides frequently or always communicated these concerns to them.

Evaluation of Local Accommodations

Overnight accommodations are a very important part of the ecotourist's experience as well as representing a significant component of the ecotourism industry. As a result, the management practices of these lodging establishments are critical to the success of ecotourism in Ecuador and other countries. To determine if nature tour operators were utilizing lodging operations that were adhering to TIES guidelines, respondents were asked to report if

Table 2.6: Tour Operator Impact Management Programme

	Never %	*Rarely* %	*Some-time* %	*Frequently* %	*Always* %
Encouraged proper behaviour in sensitive zones (n=561)	2.0	1.8	4.8	21.2	70.2
Communicated to tour group member about the need for environmental and cultural sensitivity (n=568)	1.9	2.5	9.3	34.0	52.3
Monitored tour group members behaviour during the tour (n=558)	3.2	3.8	12.4	25.4	55.2
Explained physical difficulty prior to each segment of the tour (n=558)	4.5	5.0	11.5	19.7	59.3
Encouraged proper disposal of waste products (n=552)	5.3	4.9	10.5	21.0	58.3
Cooperated with and respect of community leaders (n=412)	9.7	4.1	7.3	21.1	57.8
Explained concerns of the local communities (n=487)	7.4	8.6	16.8	26.7	40.5

they observed eight environmentally and culturally friendly actions and policies at all of the properties they stayed at. Based on all visits/stays (N=1772) at all types of accommodations (*i.e.,* hotels/lodges/yachts), 94.2% of the respondents reported that the accommodations did not keep or bait enhangered or exotic animals on the grounds. Over one-half (54.2%) of the respondents indicated that the property had adapted to the local environment. However, for the remainder of the actions and policies, respondents reported seeing them implemented at local accommodations less than one-half of the time. Overall, it appears that nature based tour operators are utilizing local lodging establishments that fail to consistently meet a majority of TIES objectives for accommodations.

Table 2.7: Evaluation of Local Accommodations

	*Frequency**	*Percentage***
Adapted to the local natural environment	961	54.2
Had informative/educational materials available for guests	790	44.6
Reflected cultural motifs through interior and/or exterior design	728	41.1
Avoided Styrofoam, plastic and excessive use of paper products	686	38.8
Sold locally produced crafts and food items on premise	587	33.1
Provided check list and guides to species found locally	503	28.4
Had a program to re-use/reduce waste.	439	24.8
Kept or baited endangered/exotic species on grounds for viewing	103	5.8

* Refers to the total number of times a particular characteristic was circled based on all visits to all accommodations . (n=1772)

** Totals more than 100% due to multiple responses.

Additional Findings

For the most part, the green evaluation was designed

to measure nature tour operators' compliance with TIES's Ecotourism Guidelines for Nature Tour Operators. However, a number of questions were asked which provide valuable insight into the attitudes and opinions of Ecuadorean ecotourists about their impact as a visitor, the importance of compliance with TIES guidelines and how to encourage compliance by nature tour operators. First, ecotourists' were asked to report how much contact (*i.e.*, none, some, a fair amount, quite a bit, a lot) they believed they had with local cultures, the majority of respondents indicated that they had some (43.5%) or a fair amount (28.3%) of contact with local cultures. Interestingly, when ecotourists were asked if their visit was intrusive into the lives of the local population, three-fourths (76.0%) responded in the negative. Second, when asked if the TIES guidelines that were discussed throughout the questionnaire should be enforced, 91.4% responded in the affirmative. For those who indicated that the guidelines be enforced, 31.9% of the respondents advocated extremely strict enforcement, 18.9% reported somewhat strict enforcement, and less than two percent (1.9%) stated leniently enforced guidelines. However, the most popular response was from the 45.7% of the respondents who felt that the enforcement of TIES guidelines depended on the circumstances.

Table 2.8: The Level of Contact Respondents had with Local Cultures

	Frequency	*Percentage*
None	59	10.3
Some	249	43.5
A Fair Amount	162	28.3
Quite a Bit	75	13.1
A Lot	27	4.7

Table 2.9: Compliance Techniques recommended by Respondents

	Frequency	*Percentage**
Suspension of operating license	288	52.1
Fear of loss of business	288	52.1
Threat of publicity, tourist finding out	242	43.8
Heavy fine	147	26.6
Fear of being prosecuted	104	18.8
Fear of being detected	54	9.8
Light fine	52	9.4
Other	53	9.5

* Totals more than 100% due to multiple responses.

Lastly, respondents were asked to indicate what methods should be used to encourage operators to follow these recommended practices. As can be seen in Table 2.9, respondents reported that the suspension of operating license (52.1%), fear of loss of business (52.1%) and threat of publicity (*i.e.*, the tourists finding out) (43.8%) were the preferred methods of encouraging nature tour operators to follow the recommended practices as suggested in this study. Moderate support was expressed for heavy fines (26.6%) and fear of being prosecuted (18.8%). Least supportive techniques were the fear of being detected (9.8%) and a light fine (9.4%).

Discussion

Results of the Green Evaluations Survey revealed a considerable amount of information about the compliance of nature tour operators with the TIES Guidelines. Information was generated regarding nature tour operators' compliance with nine out of the ten TIES guidelines. As a whole, the Green Evaluations survey does provide TIES as well as the EEA with valuable data about the current state of compliance with TIES guidelines for Ecuadorean nature tour operators. The survey results provide a year and a half snapshot of how well the Ecuadorean nature tourism industry has adhered to TIES's guiding principles of sustainable ecotourism. With this information, the EEA will be able to identify what TIES guidelines are being followed and which ones need to be given greater attention by the nature tour operators.

Findings from this survey may also be used as a benchmark for TIES and EEA to evaluate the status of compliance with nature tour operator guidelines in the future. By monitoring on a yearly basis, the EEA and TIES can determine if improvements in compliance are being made over time. While the assessment of individual businesses is limited, it is our belief that comparative analysis can be conducted that examines the differences in compliance among small, medium and large nature tour operators. This information could also be used by TIES and EEA in educating and encouraging nature tour operators of different sizes to focus on those guidelines that businesses of their size are not in compliance with.

The results of the Green Evaluations Survey revealed Ecuadorean nature tour operators are generally complying with the TIES guidelines. However, a number of areas that need to be addressed by the EEA in their pre-departure information, and visitor information and education provided during the trip include:

(1) more information about transporting alien plants, animals and disposable products,

(2) better communications regarding appropriate interactions with local residents *(i.e.,* begging, purchasing products),

(3) emphasising the importance of respecting local culture, customs, and values. Nature tour operators need to be more active in local development programmes and then communicating their actions to the customers. In addition, nature tour operators need to encourage consumers how they can get actively involved in, or contribute to, local community development programmes, Finally, one of the major areas that compliance with TIES Guidelines was poor with local accommodations. Consumers reported that local lodging establishments failed to meet many of the established guidelines. This finding has implications for both nature operators as well as the accommodations organisations in Ecuador. Specifically, nature tour operators and organisations may have to put greater pressure on lodging establishments to comply with guidelines along with lodging associations providing continuing educational programmes on appropriate environmental practices.

Future use of the Green Evaluations Process

It was felt by the researchers that the use of a consumers as a method to examine compliance with TIES guidelines was a worth and beneficial endeavour. It provides a unique perspective to the process of measuring compliance and encourage participants to get more active in the ecotourism evaluation process. It was felt that if a consumer approach to measuring nature operator compliance with TIES Guidelines is to be replicated in other countries or regions by ecotourism and travel organizations, three significant specific areas must be addressed:

(1) the length and complexity of the questionnaire used,

(2) the survey administration process, and

(3) the level of communication between researchers,

administrative agency, business owners and managers and tour guides (Higgins, 1996).

As an academic exercise, an eight page survey provided very detailed information amount nature tour operators' compliance with established ecotourism guidelines. However, it is recommended that future applications of this model utilize a shorter survey instrument that could be administered and completed more effectively buy tour guides and consumers. It appears that the questionnaire should be simplified and shortened to ease administration by guides or field representatives and completion by ecotourists. It is our recommendation that a shortened instrument be developed which addresses the nature tour guidelines in a more direct fashion. In addition, further research and discussion is needed to determine what level of compliance is acceptable? For example, should compliance to the guidelines be a minimum rating of 75 or 80%? Another question is should nature tour operators be required to have an acceptable compliance rate for each guideline or should it be based on an overall score? For the purpose of this pilot study, the seven nature tour operators who administered and returned 30 or more completed questionnaires will be able to compare their clients' evaluation of their compliance and performance with an aggregate measure of all of the tour operators.

A potentially larger problem that organizations involved in the consumer evaluation process may face is the survey instruments being administered inconsistently throughout the study period by representatives of the nature tour operators. This is evident by the five nature tour operators that did not return any completed survey instruments and the six nature tour operators who returned five or less completed or partially completed questionnaires. Unfortunately, many nature tour operators failed to follow established administration and collection procedures developed by Clemson University and TIES and directed by the EEA. To overcome this problem, it is recommended that a nature tour operator dedicate an individual who is responsible for the survey administration. This may include using a college or university student to be responsible for the data collection procedures. Finally, there was evidence from discussion with representatives from EEA and TIES that nature tour operators differed in how they administered the questionnaire. This leads researchers to conclude that communication problems may have existed between researchers, agencies, owners and managers of the nature tour operations and their field staff (*i.e.,* guides).

While tour operators recognized the value of the consumer evaluation process and were interested in participating in the study, significant problems in the administration of the survey instrument in the field was due to poor communications between business management and guides. Because guides were often preoccupied with their primary responsibilities, not well informed on the importance of the study and the need to follow established protocol or were not interested in participating in the process, the administration and collection of questionnaires on a consistent basis fell to the wayside. It is recommended that if a similar evaluation technique is undertaken in the future, a sampling process be developed in cooperation with nature tour guides that best fits their trip schedules and meets the requirements for a valid evaluation process. Finally, while an American University conducting the study meets the need of a neutral outside third party, the combination of distance, language, and cultural differences led to problems associated with data collection. It recommended that future compliance research be conducted in conjunction with a university or research institution within Ecuador. This would allow for greator on-site inspection and observation of research practices and the removal of language or cultural barriers that may negatively affect the administration and collection of compliance data.

Recommendations

It is our recommendation that given thc general support for the establishment of industry wide guidelines and the willingness of nature tour operators to participate in this evaluation process, greater attention needs to be given to all parties involved in different aspects of the study. This would include greater communication between all agencies, associations, tour operators, and guides involved that stresses the importance of their respective roles. Further, the ecotourists need to understand the value of participating in this evaluation programme. This requires them being told how the findings will be used and how they will benefit, as well as the environment and local culture, from nature tour operators adhering to management standards and guidelines. One way to accomplish this goal is through an incentive programme that encourages nature tour operators, guides, and lodging establishments to participate in the evaluation process. If the goal of the ecotourism evaluation process is a comprehensive assessment of the compliance with established ecotourism guidelines, it is also our conclusion that consumer evaluations may not be the only method utilised to evaluate the compliance of nature tour operators with industry standards and goals. While the observation and opinions of ecotourists are important and are a reasonable way to measure compliance with nature tour operator guidelines, there are a number of limitations inherent with this evaluation method alone. These problems may include: (1) The inability for consumers to accurately assess compliance with ecotourism guidelines, (2) possible confusion surrounding the terminology (*i.e.,* jargon) used in the ecotourism industry, (3) the potential for nature tour operators to censor negative evaluations by removing poor evaluations and (4) the reliance on guides to administer and collect questionnaires on a regular schedule.

Therefore, it is our recommendation that other evaluation techniques be incorporated in measuring the compliance of nature tour operators with TIES guidelines. One area of recommendation on improving the measure of compliance with TIES guidelines is the use of a knowledgeable outside party (Welsh, 1996). Specifically, the use of a third party in

(1) reviewing quality and accuracy of pre-departure information,

(2) reviewing quality and accuracy of visitor information and education provided during the trip, an evaluation of local accommodation is swwage systems and recycling programmes, and

(3) an environmental impact assessment. In addition, the author recommends that contributions to conservation and local development programmes by ecotourism operators be reported by those receiving the contributions. The technique of using multiple evaluation methods, known as itriangulation, has the advantage of measuring compliance with guidelines from a variety of perspectives.

Other methods to measure compliance could include:

(1) A peer review of the business operation and tours by a select panel from the industry,

(2) outside experts in the field of ecotourism inspecting the nature tour operators operations through a series of on-site inspection and review of appropriate business documentation,

(3) ecotourism experts participating in nature tours, this would include a combination of observation, in-depth interviews with participants and guides, and the administration of evaluation forms (*i.e.*, questionnaires) to clients, and

(4) ecotourism experts posing as customers participating

in nature tours. This form of mystery shoppers' has been used extensively in customer service satisfaction evaluation in a variety of hospitality and tourism businesses.

Lastly, it is recommended that consumer perspective be incorporated into a formal accreditation programme, like that developed in Australia, to ensure that established ecotourism standards and guidelines are being met by nature tour operators. This programme would be administered by a third party such as the Ecuadorean Ecotourism Association or possibly a government agency. The accreditation process would include a combination of:

(a) A business self-study,

(b) supporting documentation (*i.e.*, business plan, operating guidelines, evidence of economic contributions),

(c) peer review by a trained evaluation team.

(d) established guidelines on standardised testing, certification and continuing education for nature tour operator owners, managers and guides,

(e) the issuance of formal operating permit,

(f) scheduled reaccreditation procedures and standards.

In conclusion, as the ecotourism industry continues to grow, greater pressure will be placed on nature tour operators, lodging establishments, trade associations and governmental bodies to ensure a high quality tourism experience for its customers, to protect the natural and cultural resources that are utilised, and remain economically sustainable. To accomplish this goal, the ecotourism industry in countries, regions and destination areas are going to have to make tough decisions regarding how they hope to ensure the future of the industry. An underlying tension will always exists among the different ecotourism providers on how to best achieve this goal. The tension is between self-regulation by a business, the collective development and enforcement of objectives and guidelines by an ecotourism association or through regulation by a governmental entity. It is believed that TIES Green Evaluations technique.described in this paper is a process that could be incorporated by business, organisation and government agency. However, it was felt that to be a valid and reliable evaluation technique that greater controls and structures are incorporated in the data collection process.

REFERENCES

Cecil, H.O. (1995). 'The search for standards.' *EcoTraveler*, October, 1995, 16-21.

Eagles, P.F.J. (1992), 'The Travel motivations of Canadian ecotourists.' *Journal of Travel Research*, 31 (2), 3-7.

Ecotourism Association of Australia, The (1996). *National Ecotourism Accreditation Programme*. Red Hill, OLD: The Ecotourism Association of Australia.

Ecotourism Society, The (1993). *Ecotourism: A Guide for Planners & Managers*. North Bennington, VT: The Ecotourism Society.

Farrell, B.H., & Runyan, D. (1991). *Ecology and Tourism Annals of Tourism Research*, 18 (1), 26-40.

Goodale, B., & Cater, E. (1996). 'Self-regulation for sustainable tourism?' *Ecodecision*, 20, (Spring), 43-45.

Higgins, B. (1996). *Personal communication*.

Hiller, H. (1991). 'Environmental bodies edge closer to green ratings for travel.' *The International Ecotourism Society*. Newsletter, Summer, 1.

Jarvie, L. (1991). 'Responsible marketing of adventure travel and eco-tourism.' *In Proceedings of the 1991 World Congress on Adventure Travel and Eco-Tourism*. The Adventure Travel Society Inc., Englebrook, Colorado, 68-70.

Kretchman, J.A. & Eagles, P.F.J. (1990). 'An analysis of the motives of ecotourists in comparison to the general Canadian population.' *Society and Leisure,* 13 (2), 499-507.

Orams, M.B. (1995). 'Towards a more desirable form of Ecotourism.' *Tourism Management,* 16 (1), 3-8.

Scace, R.C., Grifone, E. & Usher, R. (1992). 'Ecotourism in Canada.' *Canada Environmental Advisory Council,* Environment Canada, Hull, Quebec.

Shores, J.N. (1992). The challenge of ecotourism: A call for higher standards. Paper presented at the 4th World Congress on National Parks and Protected Areas. Caracas, Venezuela, February 10-21.

Wallace, G.N., & Pierce, S.M. (1996). 'An Evaluation of Ecotourism in Amazonas, Brazil.' *Annals of Tourism Research,* 24 (4), 843-873.

Western, D. (1993). Defining Ecotourism. In *Ecotourism: A Guide for Planners & Managers,* K. Lindberg & D.E., Hawkins (Eds.), North Bennington, VT: The Ecotourism Society, 7-11.

Wight, P. (1993). 'Ecotourism: Ethics or eco-sell?' *Journal of Travel Research,* 31 (3), 3-9.

CHAPTER THREE

Nature Tourism and Environmental Impacts

Comparing the overall benefits and costs of protected areas and nature tourism enterprises can provide useful information. But there is growing acknowledgement that many of the benefits of conserving wildlife go to the world as a whole, while the costs are usually borne at national and local levels (McNeely 1988; Wells 1992). These costs usually result from loss of access to protected lands and damage caused by wildlife. The heaviest burden tends to be borne by poorer countries and especially by impoverished people living in rural areas of these countries in the proximity of protected areas. This often proves a powerful disincentive to local support for conservation, and many parks and reserves are unlikely to be able to secure their future without finding a significant role to play in supporting local social and economic development (McNeely & Miller 1984; Wells 1992). Improving relations between protected areas and neighbouring communities has therefore become one of the highest priorities on the international conservation agenda. This has led to increasing efforts by protected area managers and conservation organisations to obtain local cooperation, and to the introduction of what Wells & Brandon (1992) have referred to as integrated conservation-development projects (ICDPs). In principle there are a variety of tangible ways in which local communities could receive greater benefits from protected area tourism.

The Annapurna Conservation Area in Nepal is one of the few examples where there are signs of effective integration between tourism, local economic development and protected area management. About 40,000 people of diverse ethnic backgrounds inhabit this rugged, mountainous region, mostly poor rural farmers. Tourism has grown rapidly and 45,000 foreign trekkers now visit the area each year, virtually all of them travelling along one of two trails and there has been a proliferation of small tea shops and lodges in villages along these trails. Management of the Annapurna Conservation Area Project (ACAP) has been delegated to the King Mahendra Trust for Nature Conservation, Nepal's pre-eminent NGO. ACAP has encouraged local participation in natural resource management. Discussions with local people had revealed that establishment of a national park would meet hostility based on the fear of substantial local costs as well as skepticism towards the prospect of local economic benefits (a reaction amply justified by the history of many of Nepal's other protected areas), and an alternative was needed. Special legislation established the multiple-use Conservation Area-permitting hunting, collection of forest products and the delegation of management authority to the village level. High priority has been given to reducing the environmental impact of visiting trekkers and increasing the local economic benefits from tourism. ACAP has been authorized to collect- and retain – a visitor entry fee, helping the conservation project to become financially self-sufficient. The Government does not provide any staff or funds to manage this protected area (Wells 1993, 1994).

In another positive example, tourism at Costa Rica's Monteverde Cloud Forest Biological Preserve has had a substantial positive economic influence on the local community. The two neighbouring towns contain over 30 well-established hotels. Over 90% of visitors stay in these local hotels, for an average of two nights, and patronise local shops and restaurants. In addition, tourists use local tour agencies, gas stations, outfitters and souvenir shops, and visit the local çheese factory, sugar mill, art gallery and butterfly farm. Virtually all of these enterprises are locally owned, and a community-wide planning process helps to maintain balance between local development and management of the Preserve (Aylward *et. al.* 1996).

Ways for communities to receive greater benefits from protected are tourism

---

1. Compensation or restitution for park-caused problems
   Land claims by the dispossessed
   Damage and injuries caused by wild animals

2. Direct financial benefits for local individuals and organisations

   Revenue sharing (from hunting, culling or other plant/ animal product sales)
   Employment
   Purchasing more goods and contracting more services locally

3. Use of natural resources in parks or in buffer zones
   Hunting
   Livestock grazing
   Collection of natural products (medicinal plants, wood, construction materials, etc.)

4. Direct participation in tourism enterprises
   Employment
   Revenue sharing and joint ventures
   Selling goods and services directly to tourists-see Healey (1994)
   New market niches emphasizing traditional cultures
   Providing affordable services to low-income visitors

5.	Institutional support for community projects (schools, clinics, roads, etc.) Fund raising Direct financial support Facilitation (enlisting other government agencies and NGOs for support) Technical expertise
6.	Capacity building Training individuals with the skills needed for employment and small businesses Supporting local institutional development

Source: Adapted from Wells (1996).

But other cases are less positive. In Ecuador, many residents of the Galapagos Islands have found it difficult to benefit from ecotourism. Recent trends suggest the Galapagos are becoming a premium nature tourism destination, visited mainly by well-off people. Fewer Ecuadorians and fewer foreign backpackers seem to be visiting the islands, possibly in response to affluent residents of more wealthy nations seems to be price-inelastic. The earnings of many hotels, shops and restaurants are diminishing as the Ecuadorian and foreign backpacking visitors who tended to patronize on-shore facilities are being displaced by the gentrification of tourism. Power and water services are superior to other Ecuadorian coastal towns but prices are high, especially for food and consumer goods which must come from the mainland. Less than 15% of foreigners' expenditures are estimated to reach the islands. Most affluent visitors prefer to cruise on a ship, requiring few local inputs. Higher minimum wages and restrictive work rules for Galapagos residents means that few are employed on these ships (Southgate 1996).

In practice, local benefits from nature tourism have often been limited to employment on a very modest scale, with most tourism benefits leaking out to the national or international level. Some of the most important constraints facing increased local involvement in tourism, including community-based tourism enterprises, are the lack of required skills and experience, lack of access to markets, lack of capital for investment, lack of legal tenure or ownership rights over tourism attractions, inability to compete with larger enterprises, lack of official recognition or support for the informal sector and simple lack of financial viability (Ashley 1995). Few countries have systematically attempted to address or overcome these constraints.

One of the most significant barriers to community involvement in tourism is the lack of affordable financing. Without low-interest financing through direct and workable mechanisms, rural communities' opportunities to participate in tourism ventures are likely to remain very limited. Community participation in nature tourism may best be achievable through joint ventures with the private sector or park management authorities. This will often require capacity building in the communities, a potential role for NGOs.

Communities are generally in a very different situation from tourism industry entrepreneurs in deciding what kind of tourism product they wish to offer. In a demand- or industry-driven framework, commercial operators choose a particular tourism product based on an assessment of the potential market demand for such services in a given region. But in the supply – or capacity-driven model most relevant to communities, potential tourism enterprises must identify those services they are able to offer tourists based on local resources and then attempt to market these products. The former, demand-driven, approach is important for minimising the risk of financial failure and for exploiting untapped market potential; the latter, supply-driven approach helps ensure an enterprise is feasible, fits the local physical, ecological and cultural context and develops the local and national comparative advantage. But limited access to information, skills and capital can make it difficult for aspiring community-levels providers for aspring community-levels providers of tourism services to meet the demands of the established industry (Ashley and Garland 1994). Communities can also suffer from a lack of information about tourist markets and other local suppliers, leading to examples of over-production of local handicrafts in different communities within a region which are targeting the same groups of tourists.

Ashley & Garland (1994) recently compared the potential benefits from four types of wildlife tourism enterprise in communal areas in Namibia

(i) a privately-owned lodge;

(ii) a privately-owned lodge voluntarily sharing revenue with the community;

(iii) a joint venture lodge, usually where the community owns the land and is entitled to lease payments or profit-sharing in a privately-run lodge on their land; and

(iv) a community owned and managed tourism enterprise (*e.g.*, campsites, craft sales or cultural attractions).

This study concluded that an up-market lodge will usually make a larger contribution to the regional or national economy simply because of its scale, although the community enterprise's contribution can also be sustainable if the social benefits of skill acquisition, institutional development, and equity of benefit distribution are valued in economic terms. But if the four different enterprises are ranked according to the revenue which they generate for a community, then a joint venture lodge is preferable, followed by community enterprises, then revenue-sharing private lodges. But even a private lodge which does not share revenues can inject income into the community through employee wages (Ashley and Garland 1994). Joint venture lodges appear to offer

---

Factors influencing the feasibility of community involvement in nature tourism

The financial viability of any tourism lodge in a communal area depends on the tourism product, prices, occupancy rates, and the balance between government taxes and government services (roads, water, power, airports).

The scale of communitie's benefits and costs from private lodges depends on the number of local jobs and wage levels, and the local resources used by the lodge.

The feasibility of revenue-sharing from a private lodge depends on:

- Overall lodge profitability
- The extent to which revenue-sharing costs can be passed on to customers, perhaps by attracting specialized tourists with an ethical/ecological focus.
- The value of reciprocal benefits to the tourism enterprise from the community (goodwill, resource conservation, land-use agreements).
- Awareness among entrepreneurs and communities of potential mechanisms and benefits of revenue-sharing.
- Government incentives (taxes, subsidies, promotion, publicity).

The feasibility of establishing joint ventures between communities and entrepreneurs depends on:

- The extent to which above-above-average prices can be charged to compensate entrepreneurs for giving up a share of profit and achieving a lower return on their investment.
- The value of community rights over tourism resources (wildlife and land).
- Transaction costs of negotiating and establishing joint ventures, and the extent to which NGOs and government can help reduce these (*e.g.*, by providing expertise).
- Awareness, interest and objectives of entrepreneurs and communities.

The feasibility of country enterprises depends on:

- Prices and occupancy/usage rates (which depend on competitors as well as promotion and marketing).

- Secure access to a valuable site.
- Skills in business, languages, marketing, management, and so on.
- Changes in local land use and tourism development which are beyond the community's ability to influence.
- Availability of capital.

Source: Adapted from Ashley & Garland (1994).

the best chance of strengthening the critical linkage between community development and wildlife conservation. Only a joint venture lodge seems likely to generate benefits which are sufficiently large and widely dispersed to be perceived as depending on wildlife conservation. A community enterprise could have similar effects but the financial benefits would be smaller. Opportunities for active community participation and empowerment are greatest in community enterprises and joint ventures, while the community's role in revenue sharing tends to be passive. A private lodge without revenue sharing generally does little to encourage community participation (Ashley 1995; Ashley & Garland 1994). Even when significant revenues for the community are generated by tourism, deciding how to distribute these revenues within a community presents a further challenge.

Mitigating Nature Tourism's Environmental Impacts

An economic approach to the management of protected areas and other nature tourism destinations can help to identify ways of maximizing net financial or economic benefits. But one of the most important challenges in managing tourism is to reach a balance between the benefits from visitor use and the maintenance of the natural environmental features of the area. When the use of a nature tourism destination is uncontrolled, maximising net economic benefits may result in irreversible damage to the environment. The market system would be likely to deliver to many tangible benefits at the expense of intangibles, such as non-use benefits (Driml & Common 1995).

So the economic solution poses a dilemma for destination managers. The dilemma arises because the economic approach sets values based on the summed preferences of individuals' willingness to pay, and these are unlikely to coincide with the social and political values which generally underlie the establishment of conservation priorities. The optimal economic solution will probably only coincide with the conservation objectives of a protected area when constraints are added to maintain a defined standard of environmental quality (Driml & Common 1995).

Limitation of visitor numbers is perhaps the most obvious met' ·d for managing negative impacts and this has led to a focus on ecological carrying capacity within the tourism literature (Lindberg *et. al.* 1996). (Ecological carrying capacity can be contrasted with economic carrying capacity where net economic value is maximized, as discussed in section 5.) Unfortunately, the many definitions offered for a destination's ecological carrying capacity provide little useful guidance for practical implementation. For example, carrying capacity has been defined as "the level of visitor use an area can accommodate with high levels of satisfaction for visitors and few impacts on resources" (WTO/UNEP 1992), cited in Lindberg *et. al.* 1996). It is unclear what constitutes either "high levels" or "few impacts".

Carrying capacity might be a more useful concept if the negative environmental impact of visitors was a linear or other simple function of some easily-measured variable, such as the number of visitors. Then carrying capacity could be defined reliably in terms of that variable. But, as Aylward and colleagues (1996) have argued, in reality environmental deterioration due to tourism overuse often occurs in mysterious increments so that predicting or assessing the point at which irreversible damage begins is a difficult task. Given the problem of determining environmental thresholds calculating the exact carrying capacity of a nature tourism attraction is often not feasible.

Recognition that effective application of the carrying capacity concept is difficult, if not impossible, has led to a shift in focus from the "how many is too many?" question to one of "what are the desired (social and environmental) conditions?" (Lindberg *et al.* 1996). This shift in emphasis has led to the development of alternative planning and management frameworks, including the Limits of Acceptable Change system, Visitor Impact Management and Visitor Experience Resource Protection. Lindberg *et al.* (1996) cite references which gives details of these iterative frameworks, which allow for the identification of use-impact relationships.

In the Monteverde Cloud Forest Biological Preserve, Costa Rica, visitor numbers are limited during the two annual peak visitation periods, to 100 people at a time on the 20 km of visitor trails which cover a small fraction of the reserve, and these trails are periodically moved. Visitors are not permitted to step off the designated paths and, if acute deterioration is noted, trails are closed for restoration. This approach combines careful monitoring with adaptive management. The non-profit Preserve was originally intended to protect nature and provide a site for biological research. It remains to be seem what action will be taken if the 100-person limit becomes a binding constraint on visitor numbers and revenue generation. A commercially-operated reserve would presumably solve this constraint by extending the trail network. One alternative would be to simply cap development and let other private reserves take the overflow (Aylward *et. al.* 1996).

But tourism impacts can be very diverse and difficult to monitor. For example, the types of impact identified for the Great Barrier Reef World Heritage Area in Australia include: site impacts from structures, mooring and anchorings; coral damage from diving and reef walking; removal of coral and shells; garbage disposal and littering; sediment disturbance and dredging; water pollution from nutrients, heavy metals and oil; sewage discharge from vessels and from island resorts; fishing impacts; fish feeding impacts; and impacts of research and monitoring activities (Driml & Common in press). Monitoring such a wide range of variables and adjusting visitor numbers and activities in response to the results of such monitoring is obviously a massive and expensive management undertaking.

Damage done is not just as a result of the *volume* of tourists (taking into account both numbers and length of visit), but also as a result of the *damage done per tourist* (Steele 1995). This means that carrying capacity (however defined) can be increased by investing in more effective management to mitigate damage (Swanson 1992, cited in Steele 1995). Improved management might, for example, include increasing spatial and temporal dispersion of tourists (or even concentration of visitors in resilient or even already damaged areas). For example, Medio (1996) showed how educating divers in advance on the fragility of coral reefs led to significant reductions in damage per diver at a Egyptian diving resort. Dixon *et. al.* (1995) reported similar findings from the Bonaire Marine Park, suggesting that it may be possible to double the estimated present usage level of 2,00,000 dives per year with improved management and more effective dives education.

Private sector tourism operators will only have an incentive to support and invest in additional management to reduce environmental damage where market access is limited and regulated. If market access is unlimited or unregulated, free riders-operators who decline to incur the extra costs of additional management – will still be able to share in the benefits without regard for environmental damage, and the incentive to cooperate and reduce environmental damage for the common good will be lost. Kenya's Maasai Mara National reserve provides an example. Illegal, but virtually unregulated, off-road driving by tour operator vehicles anxious to provide their clients with close-up wildlife views have significantly scarred the landscape. Together with the failure to limit tourist or vehicle numbers, this has led to environmental damage, modified wildlife behaviour and diminished the visitor experience.

So far the discussion has been limited to direct environmental damage to a nature tourism attraction. Indirect environmental damage is often more serious. Aylward *et. al.* (1996) refer to an unplanned development "free for all" on the fringes of some popular nature tourism destinations in Costa Rica. And, of course, most forms of transport, even to the most environmentally-sensitive ecotourism destinations, impose substantial environmental costs through air pollution and carbon dioxide emissions.

In Ecuador's Galapagos National Park, controls control on damage per tourist include careful zoning, regulations that tourists must be accommodated on boats, registration of naturalist guides and strict rules of shore visits (de Groot 1983, cited in Steele 1995). But there have been no controls on the number of tourists. The volume of visitors to this formerly-remote and isolated archipelago has increased dramatically, from about 5,000 in 1970 to more than 55,000 (40,000 foreigners) in 1995. As a result, thousands of unrestricted migrants have been attracted to the Galapagos by the prospect of working in a souvenir shop or on a cruise ship. The resident population increased from 2,400 in 1962 to almost 10,000 in 1990. The towns are now sources of pollution. Many of the residents do not succeed in finding permanent work and take up fishing. This is unregulated and several fish species have been severely depleted, with unknown effects on the local food chain (Southgate 1996).

Environmental damage to a nature tourism destination should ideally be monitored with reference to carefully-selected environmental indicators, which wil usually be site-specific and will often be difficult to measure. 'Leading' indicators to identify impending environmental damage are most needed. Adaptive management of visitors in response to the signals from such careful and regular monitoring would ideally focus on infrastructure and other development as well as visitor numbers, duration of stay and activities. Unfortunately, few developing country nature tourist attractions have the financial or institutional capacity to manage tourism in such a sophisticated fashion. In the absence of such capabilities, local expert opinion backed up with the legal authority and institutional capacity to regulate may be the next-best option. Economic analysis and instruments become most useful in helping to work out how to extract the maximum net benefits from tourism once the acceptable environmental conditions have been defined.

Nature Tourism Future Research

Economic studies of nature tourism in developing countries were few and far between as recently as five years ago. But important progress has recently been made in demonstrating nature tourism's significant contribution to several countries' economies, and in showing that nature tourism can generate substantial economic benefits. One clear result has been the growing tendency for protected areas and some other nature tourism destinations to increase user fees, to try to capture a greater share of these economic benefits. Some progress has also been made in demonstrating that gains in economic and environmental efficiency can result from regulating development and use at nature tourism destinations, although unequivocal examples remain limited. Practical efforts to regulate private sector operators' access to nature tourism attractions, to avoid either unlimited entry or dominant and inefficient cartels, remain rare.

Nature tourism has complex and important linkages with a wide range of environmental and developmental processes across several different sectors. But a comprehensive analytical synthesis of the lessons from experience and their implications for government policymaking has yet to be carried out, even in a single country. So far even the most technically sophisticated and insightful studies of one or a few aspects of nature tourism have generally proven insufficient as a basis for helping developing country governments identify and evaluate their overall nature tourism policy options.

There appear to be two main reasons why nature tourism research studies have generally had only a modest influence on government policymaking. First, very little research has been policy-oriented. Financial resources for research have often been limited and these resources have often been mobilized by academic researchers who are more interested in testing a specific methodological approach rather than broad sets of policy questions. Even when supported by international development agencies, such research has tended to focus on theoretical aspects of single issues, such as destination entry fee policies, or on general thematic reviews unsupported by detailed analysis. Relatively few researchers have been able to access useful data on private sector tourism operations. As a result of these constraints, practical policy recommendations usable by government decision-makers have typically not emerged, even in the most-studied countries such as Costa Rica and Kenya.

The second reasons is related to the diverse priorities and expectations of the different stakeholder groups with an interest in nature tourism. Finance and economic planning ministries usually perceive the opportunities in terms of foreign exchange earnings, jobs and economic growth; conservation agencies in terms of increased park entry fees (offset by new management challenges); commercial tourism operators and private landowners in terms of financial profit; and local communities in terms of jobs and opportunities for local businesses, NGO expectations depend on their orientation but often combine local community and conservation agency views. Understandably, these stakeholders have very diverse views on the most appropriate policy and institutional arrangements for achieving their own sets of goals. Very few financial or economic studies of nature tourism have seriously attempted to understand, let alone measure, the impacts of different policy options on more than one of these diverse stakeholder groups.

Efforts to develop effective national policies for nature tourism have thus been frustrated by the lack of prioritized economic analysis of the options as well as the need to appreciate and reconcile the diverse stakeholder perspectives. This indicates the need for applied economic research in selected case study countries which is not only targeted to provide usable insights but also sufficiently grounded in an appreciation of the perspectives of the various stakeholders to produce results which are usable in cross-sectoral governmental decision-making. In other words, finding more effective ways for stakeholder involvement to be combined with technical analysis for policy development.

The remainder of this section consists of sets of an overall menu of key research questions for evaluating options and strategies for optimizing the economic and ecological benefits associated with nature tourism. Country-specific policy research could prioritize from such a menu.

Definition and Characterisation

- How can nature tourism best be defined or characterized as a subset of all domestic and international tourism?
- Who owns and determines access rights to nature tourism destinations?
- What is the structure of the nature tourism industry, who are the key actors and how has the industry

developed?

Which government departments or ministries have a significant direct or indirect impact (or potential impact) on nature tourism?

Definition and characterization of nature tourism in case study countries will be an important first step before a detailed research programme is undertaken (B. Aylward, personal communication). Characterization is likely to involve several different aspects of nature tourism: the type of ecosystem (*e.g.*, semi-arid areas, coral reefs, wetlands, tropical forests, mountain areas), the types of commercial operations comprising the industry (size, distribution, horizontal and vertical linkages, ownership, relationships with 'mainstream' tourism, and so on), the types of visitors (*e.g.*, countries of origin, income levels, types of experiences sought), ownership and management arrangements of the nature tourism destinations (national conservation agencies, provincial conservation agencies, NGOs, private sector, indigenous communities, and so on), and the key government departments or ministries.

Measurement

- What have been the principal economic impacts of nature tourism, and how have these impacts been distributed geographically?
- What financial and economic benefits and costs (including opportunity costs) have been associated with nature tourism, both directly and indirectly, and how are these benefits distributed at local, national and international levels?

Estimates of the economic impacts of tourism have usually been considerably more influential over government decision-making than estimates of the economic benefits and costs. The former requires an estimate of the magnitude of financial transactions attributable to tourism destinations while the latter requires an economic welfare analysis.

Other important measurement questions include:

- What financial and economic rates of return have been earned by the major types of nature tourism enterprises?
- What government revenues have been generated by nature tourism?
- What have been the principal government policies and instruments for encouraging or regulating nature tourism, and what impact have these had?
- How have the financial and economic viability of nature tourism been affected by government intervention (*e.g.*, taxes and subsidies) in sectors which are competing land use options, such as agriculture, forestry or mining?

Policy Issues

Policy issues on which research is needed include:

- What are the options for increasing and capturing a greater proportion of the net economic benefits associated with nature tourism (including new tourism destinations, expansion of tourism facilities at existing destinations, higher access fees and/or multiple pricing policies, reduction of leakages form the local or national economy)?
- How can nature tourism contribute more to local economic development and what are realistic options for overcoming the often significant barriers to local participation in nature tourism?
- What are the options for mitigating nature tourism's environmental impacts and how can the environmental

and social impacts of nature tourism be monitored and regulated in ways which are cost-effective and useful to protected area managers?

- What are the appropriate institutional arrangements for managing and regulating the use of nature tourism destinations (including limiting and regulating market access to destinations, privatizing state protected areas or tourism operations within these areas)?
- What are the benefits from expanding nature tourism on private lands through incentives for landowners and other mechanisms, and to what extent is tourism compatible with alternative land uses?
- What types of nature tourism should be promoted by governments under various conditions (*e.g.*, high cost/low volume vs. low cost/high volume) and what policy instruments should be used as incentives?
- What overall sets of ecological, socio-economic and institutional conditions are most likely to support nature tourism's contribution to biodiversity conservation and sustainable development?

REFERENCES

Ashley, C. & E. Garland 1994. Promoting community-based tourism development: What, why and how? Research Discussion Paper No. 4. Department of Environmental Affairs, Ministry of Environment and Tourism, Namibia.

Aylward, B., Allen, K., Echeverria, J. & J. Tosi 1996. Sustainable ecotourism in Costa Rica: The Monteverde Cloud Forest Reserve. *Biodiversity and Conservation* 5:315-343.

Barnes, J.I. 1996 (in press). *Economic characteristics of demand for wildlife viewing tourism in Botswana.* Development Southern Africa 13.

Barnes, J. & J. de Jager 1996 (in press). Economic and financial incentives for wildlife use on private land in Namibia and the implications for policy. *South African Journal of*

Wildlife Research.

Boo, E. 1990. *Ecotourism: The potentials and pitfalls,* 2 volumes. World Wildlife Fund, Washington, DC.

Brandon, K. 1996. Ecotourism and conservation: A review of the issues. Environment Department Paper No. 33. Global Environment Division, World Bank.

Briassoulis, H. 1991. Tourism input-output analysis. *Annals of Tourism Research* 18: 485-495.

CHAPTER FOUR

Economic Impact of Nature Tourism and Cultural Activities in Worcester County

Tourism is the county's number one industry, fueled in large party by Ocean City, the state's premier Atlantic oceanfront destination, attracting an estimated 10 million visitors each year. But Worcester County has many other recreational amenities and opportunities that also draw millions of visitors each year. Nature lovers and wildlife enthusiasts visit the area attracted by the natural and cultural resources: The sandy ocean beaches of Assateague Island, the quiet of the Pocomoke River and the bays, the unique wildlife including free-roaming horses and rare species of birds, and the many sporting and boating opportunities. Many also come to enjoy the county's rich cultural history, evident in the quaint towns of Berlin, Snow Hill and Pocomoke City that offer historic inns, museums, artists' galleries, shops, restaurants, and seasonal festivals. Visitors that participate in nature tourism and cultural activities are the focus of this study. The study defines nature tourism as recreational activities that focus on nature in a more pristine and remote form that is typical of a beach visit to a devleoped ocean front destination such as Ocean City.

Recreational activities of interest to this study involve the natural and cultural heritage of Worcester County and excludes the economic impact of tourism generated by Ocean City. Aside from being the home of Ocean City, Worcester County has numerous other extraordinary natural resources providing opportunities for recreational experiences that are different from what many in the local tourism industry characterize as the "typical Ocean City visit."

These include miles of pristine and undeveloped Atlantic Ocean beaches located just south of Ocean City in the Assateague Island National Seashore and Assateague State Park, as well as many outstanding coastal bay-related recreational areas and sites. Nature tourism participants in Worcester County include two types: those who are primarily visiting Ocean City but also participate in nature-based recreational activities, and those who participate only in nature-based activities and do not visit Ocean City. Ocean City visitors who also participate in nature tourism activities seek experiences that are different from their Ocean City beach visit in that they seek out recreational venues in more pristine and undeveloped areas. For example, visitors seek out Assateague Island for its undeveloped beaches, flora, and fauna or the Pocomoke River for canoeing or kayaking in a pristine and remote area.

Methodology

Money spent on nature tourism is an important part of the economy of Worcester County. Recreational spending is generated by visitors—or tourists-coming to the region from other parts of Maryland, other states, and other countries. (The terms visitors and tourists are used interchangeably in this study.) County residents—year-around residents and those who own a second home in the county-also spend money on recreation. However, due to data limitations discussed later in this report, expenditures by country residents are not included in the estimates presented in this study.

Researchers use two principal methods for estimating recreation and tourism spending and economic impacts: satellite accounts derived from national data sets and data collected from visitor surveys.

Satellite Accounts: The Bureau of Economic Analysis (BEA), the World Tourism Organisation, and other organisations have developed satellite accounts for tourism. A satellite account reorganizes the national system of accounts to identify the contribution of tourism to a state or national economy. Satellite accounts are primarily used to give an overall aggregate estimate of the contribution of tourism-related activity from a system of national accounts. The advantage of the satellite accounting approach is that it uses existing economic data and embeds tourism in an accepted system of accounts.

National accounts are organised around a set of industries or commodities. The drawback is that the information necessary to extract tourism activity from national economic accounts often is lacking. Also, satellite methods are difficult to apply below the national level or for subcategories of activities such as nature tourism. The problem is that tourism is more a type of customer than either an industry or a type of commodity. For example, restaurants serve both tourists and local residents, and the system of accounts has no way of distinguishing one from the other. The basic procedure in satellite accounting is to assign a share of sales of each commodity or industry to tourism. These shares, however, can vary widely for different regions and seasons. Because of the inability to apply national data to local situations, satellite accounts were not used for this study.

Visitor Surveys: Surveying better estimates economic impacts of tourist spending and is the approach used in this study. Due to the lack of information specific to Worcester County, a year-long visitor survey was conducted in multiple locations throughout the county, generating responses from 1,279 nature tourism participants. The survey methodology and results are discussed in detail in the next chapter.

Surveys are generally used when spending and resulting impact estimates are desired for particular markets segments (*e.g.*, nature tourism) or for local regions (*e.g.*, Worcester County). Whenever possible, spending data are gathered using visitor surveys and applied to estimates of the volume of tourism activity in an area. Spending totals are then applied to a regional economic model to estimate economic impacts on the area, usually including secondary or multiplier effects. Using the model, estimates of spending can be translated into the resulting jobs and income in a given area using appropriate economic ratios and multipliers. Economic impacts can be estimated in terms of spending, income, value added, tax revenues, and employment. The basic equations are as follows:

Tourism Spending = Number of Visitors × Average Spending/ Visitor

Economic Impact = Number of Visitors × Average Spending/

Visitor × Multiplier

The Worcester County Visitor Survey does not collect information on tourist expenditures directly. This was beyond the resources available for the study. Other methods of estimating expenditures were used, including extrapolations from existing data sources for the State of Maryland, other studies, local observations of market transactions, and expert opinion.

Some studies attempt to estimate the economic impact of non-market values and add those to market estimates to come up with an estimate of total economic impact. This study does not estimate non-market values of recreation spending. Non-market values are dollar estimates of how much people would be willing to spend for a particular recreational activity or experience but do not actually spend. For example, people may value bird-watching very highly, beyond the money they actually spend on the activity of bird-watching. A non-market approach attaches a dollar value to a day of bird-watching and includes that amount, along with all other non-market estimates, in the economic impact estimate. While non-market values may represent economic value, they are of a decidedly different nature than market values since they do not represent actual economic activity generated by visitor spending. The economic impact estimates presented in this study represent actual economic activity generated from recreation spending and the jobs supported by that spending.

Nature Tourism in Worcester County

Worcester County is home to a permanent population of nearly 47,000, which has grown by more than 30 percent since 1990.[1] It is the destination of millions of visitors annually who come to enjoy the wide variety of recreational opportunities that abound. Tourism is the county's number one industry, fueled in large part by Ocean City, the state's premier Atlantic oceanfront destination. Ocean City attracts 8 to 10 million visitors annually, with as many as 3,00,000 visitors flooding the town each week during the summer season.

But aside from Ocean City, Worcester County has many other recreational amenities and opportunities that draw millions of visitors each year. Nature lovers and wildlife enthusiasts visiting the area are attracted by the natural and cultural resources: sandy beaches, quiet rivers and bays, free-roaming horses, rare species of birds and many sporting opportunities. People also come to enjoy the county's rich cultural history, evidenced by the quaint towns that offer historic inns, museums, artists' galleries, shops, restaurants and seasonal festivals. Worcester County draws most of its visitors from nearby areas, primarily the Washington, D.C. and Baltimore metropolitan areas, Pennsylvania, Delaware, New Jersey, and New York; but many visitors travel longer distances, coming from far away states, Canada, and Europe.

More than a million visitors travel to Assateague Island each year, which is located south of the Ocean City inlet and is accessible from the mainland via Route 611.

Located on the bay side of the island are the Assateague Island National Seashore Headquarters and Visitor Center, as well as a boat launching ramp and fishing piers that are part of Assateague State Park. On the Ocean side, Assateague State Park provides access to a broad sandy beach, with changing facilities, rest rooms, and other amenities. Adjacent to the south is Assateague Island National Seashore with access to the Atlantic Ocean beach and extensive visitor amenities. The national park also provides opportunities for camping, nature trails and walks led by naturalists, as well as canoeing, kayaking, crabbing, and clamming. Visitors to Assateague Island come to enjoy the pristine beaches and the unique wildlife. Aside from approaching Assateague Island from the mainland, visitors can board tour boats in Ocean City for an "eco tour" that features the northern portion of the Assateague Island National Seashore. These tours have recently been licensed by the National Park Service. Another important destination for nature tourists is the Pocomoke River State Forest and Park, located between Snow Hill and Pocomoke City, which provides camping and boating facilities at Shad and Milburn Landings and opportunities for hiking, canoeing, and wildlife observation.

Boating is a very popular recreational activity in Worcester County. More than 4,000 pleasure boats are registered in the county and many more boats are hauled to the area by visitors attracted by many pleasure boating and sport fishing opportunities. More than 40 public boat launching ramps provide access to the coastal bays and the Pocomoke River.

Several small towns attract visitors to Worcester County because of their historic charm and quiet appeal. Berlin, located several miles inland from Ocean City, is a quaint small town characterised by a charming ambiance of period architecture, antique shops, arts and crafts galleries, and restaurants. Berlin has become a popular visitor destination since it was featured in the recent hit movie "Runaway Bride". Snow Hill, a 10 minute drive from Berlin and located on the Pocomoke River, is another pleasant and unique small town featuring period architecture and streetscapes, museums, B&Bs, boat rentals, river cruises, antique and speciality shops, and restaurants, all within easy walking distance of the historic Worcester County Court House. A boat landing, picnic area, and quaint B&B are available at Public Landing, located several miles east of Snow Hill on Chincoteague Bay. Furnace Town, located several miles west of Snow Hill, is both an outdoor museum—featuring a restored 19th century iron furnace—and the home of the popular Celtic Festival held each July. Pocomoke City, located on the Pocomoke River several miles south of Snow Hill, is another small town of appeal to visitors, including boaters who dock at the municipal marina.

The natural attractions of Worcester County include the pristine flora and fauna that provide opportunity for a myriad of recreational activities, both passive and active. Fishing is a popular sport pursued by boaters and those fishing from shore or piers. Species popular with fishermen are sea truth, bluefish, striped bass, white perch, and American shad. Crabbing and clamming are other popular recreational activities, with blue crabs and hard-shell clams most popular. Birds are another important natural resource, including seabirds, waterfowl, and wading birds. Seabirds include several species of gulls and terns. Waterfowl include Canada Geese, Black Duck, Mallard and Canvasack. Wading birds include several species of egrets and herons. Also important and unique to the area are the feral horses that roam Assateague Island.

Worcester County Visitor Survey

The decision to conduct a visitor survey in Worcester County was made early on in the project because no existing data source provides information on the characteristics of nature tourism participants in the county. The visitor surveys conducted as part of this study consisted of both administered and self-administered surveys. Administered surveys are those in which researchers approach visitors at pre-determined locations and request that the visitors participate in the survey.

Self-administered questionnaires are those that visitors pick-up at a particular site, complete, and return to a collection point. Prior to beginning the visitor survey, focus groups and meetings were held with representatives from Worcester County, the Maryland Department of Natural Resources, the National Park Service, local natural resource conservation organisations, and the local business community. The purpose of the sessions was to develop a working definition of nature tourism, including a list of there recreational activities to be included in the study, and to build local support for the project. It was important to provide information on the goals and objectives of the study and receive local input, including suggestions for the survey, possible locations for placement, and any potential difficulties in conducting the survey. As a result of these early planning sessions, both the National Park Service and the Maryland Department of Natural Resources granted permission to conduct visitor surveys within the Assateague Island National Seashore, Assateague State Park and Pocomoke River State Park. Official permission was critical since the National Seashore and Maryland state parks are the most frequently visited locations in Worcester County that are of interest to this study (i.e., outside of Ocean City) and are the focal points for nature tourism in the area. Further, local officials from three municipalities in Worcester County—the Town of Berlin, the City of Pocomoke, and the Town of Snow Hill—were consulted and in turn offered support for the project. Letters were sent out from the headquarters or local government office explaining the survey to citizens, employees, and area businesses and asking for their help in data collection.

The *Visitor Survey* questionnaire was designed by the University of Maryland Institute for Governmental Service with input from the Worcester County Tourism Office and officials from the National Park Service Assateague Island National Seachor and the Maryland Department of Natural Resources. The survey was designed to be relatively short, requiring three to five minutes to complete. Other important considerations in designing the survey were to ensure the anonymity of respondents and to be non-intrusive. No questions were asked pertaining to home address or income; the survey asked only for the zip code of the respondent's principal residence. Also, no questions were asked relating directly to visitor expenditures since such questions are intrusive to some visitors. The survey was field tested by IGS staff in both the national and state parks.

Survey questions focused on whether respondents live in Worcester County, their general location of origin (*i.e.*, state and zip code), number of people in the party, number and type of overnights, reasons for selecting overnight accommodations and recreational activities planned, whether owning or renting equipment, and in which tours they participated. Responses to these questions were compiled to develop a profile of visitors who participate in nature tourism in Worcester County, to estimate participation rates (*e.g.*, the share of visitors participating in each of the activities of interest to the study), and to provide information to be used in estimating visitor spending. Respondents also were asked to list attractions or amenities they would like to see in the area that are not currently available. This was asked not because it is directly relevant to estimating economic impact but because it provides valuable information to local officials and the business community. The same is true of information about specific establishments *i.e.*, hotels, bed & breakfasts, etc.).

Visitor surveys were conducted for one year from August 2000 through July 2001. Initially the focus was on the placement of survey displays at various locations throughout Worcester County. The display provided basic information about the survey, including who was conducting it and for what purpose. Displays were set in conspicuous locations in a variety of establishments such as restaurants, antique stores, specialty shops, hotels, bed and breakfasts, and museums. Approximately 50 initial locations had survey displays. An envelope was provided in which visitors placed their completed surveys, and the surveys were monitored on a bi-weekly basis. After monitoring the locations for approximately three months, displays were removed from a few locations that had received no completed surveys. In addition, several new locations were added.

The second phase of data collection was conducting field surveys at various locations throughout Worcester County. Field survey locations included Assateague Island National Seashore, Assateague State Park, Shad Landing State Park, Milburn Landing State Park, and Furnace Town. Field surveys began in September 2000 and continued through June 2001. Two methods of collecting field surveys were used. Surveyors would canvas a particular location (*e.g.*, Assateague State Park) and approach visitors. Surveyors would provide a brief introduction and explanation of the survey and the visitors would be asked to participate by filling out a survey. For particular events, such as Maryland Coast Day, surveyors set up a table with a sign explaining the nature of the survey, and eight to ten clipboards with surveys were available. Those who completed the survey received a small giveaway (*i.e.*, a floating key chain provided by Worcester County Tourism) for their help.

During the one-year data collection effort, a total of 1,279 visitor surveys were collected. The survey responses were entered into a Microsoft Access database and analysed using various queries. The results of the queries describing the general characteristics of visitors follow in the next section of this report. The data were also analysed to obtain information on the number of respondents participating in the various nature tourism activities. These values were used to estimate participation rates. The data tables and analyses are presented in Appendix B to this report.[2]

Results of the Worcester County Visitor Survey

Of the total number of respondents, 12 percent (157) live in Worcester County, An additional 6 percent (78) own a second home or a condo in Worcester County. These figures indicate that a significant number of Worcester County residents participate in nature tourism activities and that those owning a second home or condo are also very likely to enjoy nature tourism related activities.

Parties of two adults constituted 63 percent (790) of visitors, with parties of one to four adults constituting 95 percent of all visitors (1192).

Forty-one percent of two-adult parties traveled without children, while 16 percent of two-adult parties traveled with one or two children. The majority of three to six-adult parties traveled without children. Larger group sizes of seven or more adults are less common but not infrequent.

These are likely multi-family or school/interest groups.

Not surprisingly, nearly one-half of all visitors surveyed come to Worcester County to enjoy the seashore. Twenty-two percent of visitors (268) listed Assateague Island as the end destination of their trip, with an additional 2 percent (25) listing Chincoteague Island. Many of those traveling to Assateague or Chincoteague also listed other local attractions and events as part of their trip destination. Another 22 percent (267) listed Ocean City as their final trip destination.

Forty-four percent of visitors (700) knew about the area because they had been there before. Twenty-two percent (346) heard about the area from family or friends. Twelve percent (189) heard about Worcester County through print advertising 3 percent (48) through radio/TV advertising, and 7 percent (107) through the Internet. Twelve percent (207) listed other sources for finding out about Worcester County nature attractions, including articles in Soundings and *Southern Living* magazines, newspapers, guidebooks for various activities such as birding and canoeing, books, and "just happening by". Table 4.1 presents a conclusion of selected visitors characteristics.

TABLE 4.1
Worcester County Visitor Characteristics (Selected)

		% of Respondents
Live in Worcester County		12%
Own Second Home or Condo in County		6%
Number or Adults in Party	1 Adult	12%
	2 Adults	63%
	3-4 Adults	20%
	5-6 Adults	3%
	> 6 Adults	2%
Number of Adults and Children in Party	2 Adults 0 Children	41%

	2 Adults 1 or 2 Children	16%
End Destination of Trip	Worcester County (Non-OC)	58%
	Ocean City/Beach	22%
	Other	20%
How Visitors Heard About the Area	Have Been Here Before	44%
	Recommended	22%
	Print Advertising	12%
	Other	12%
Where Visitors Came From	Maryland	44%
	Pennsylvania	17%
	Virginia	9%
	Delaware	7%
	New Jersey	5%
	New York	5%
	International	1.5%
Type of Lodging	Campground/Cabin	33%
	Hotel/Motel	26%
	Family/Friends	20%
	Bed & Breakfast	14%
	Undisclosed	7%
Number of Overnights	0 Nights	35%
	1-2 Nights	28%
	3-6 Nights	25%
	7-13 Nights	9%
Reason for Lodging Choice 21%	Convenient to Local Attractions	
	Price	135
	On way to Other Destination	5%
	Overflow From Beach	4%
	Other	57%

Not surprisingly, 44 percent (460) of respondents came from Maryland, 17 percent (176) came from Pennsylvania, nine percent (94) from Virginia, seven percent (73) from Delaware, and five percent each from New York and New Jersey. Less than two percent (16) of visitors came from foreign countries including Canada, England, France, Germany and Hungary. Of the 68 percent (867) of respondents who said they were staying overnight in the area, 33 percent (290) stayed in a campground or cabin, 26 percent

(226) in a hotel or motel, 20 percent (176) with family or friends, and 14 percent (119) in a B&B.

One-half of visitors were visiting for short stays ranging for one to five nights. Twenty-eight percent (356) of respondents stayed one to two nights, another 23 percent (292) stayed three to five nights. Ten percent (128) stayed six to ten nights and less than two percent (21) stayed 14 nights.

Fewer than one percent (6) of the visitors stayed 100 or more nights. Twenty-one percent (263) listed "convenient to local attractions" as their reason for selecting their accommodations; another 13 percent (166) listed "price" as their reason, five percent (61) selected lodging because it was "on the way to another destination," and four percent (59) stayed in "overflow from beach locations."

Fifty-seven percent (730) of visitors gave other reasons for their choice of lodging. Most frequent among those was that they enjoy camping, particularly on the beach. Another reason often cited was that they "always come here" or "had been here before."

Visitor Participation in Nature Tourism

Estimates of spending on nature tourism require an understanding of: (1) the total number of persons who participate in nature tourism activities, and (2) the number of persons-expressed as a share of the total—who participate in the various recreational activities of interest to this study. To develop these estimates, several steps are necessary:

1. determine the total number of visitors annually to Worcester County who participate in nature tourism activities;
2. estimate the percentage of visitors engaging in each type of nature tourism activity;
3. compute the participation rate for each activity by

multiplying the total number of visitors (1) by the percentage who participate in each activity (2)

4. estimate the average dollar amount spent per participant day on each activity as well as the average cost of transportation, lodging, and food associated with each recreational activity[3];

5. calculate direct visitor spending by multiplying the participation rate (3) by the average daily spending on each activity(4).

Total Number of Visitors: Since the *Worcester County Visitor Survey* was not designed to provide information on the total number of visitors, the study looks to other existing data sources. *Travel Scope,* a firm that collects and disseminates tourism-related data for locations nationwide, estimates annual visitation to Worcester County ranging from 6 to 10 million.[4] No breakout of visitors to Ocean City versus other locations in the county is available. *Travel Scope* defines a visitor as someone who travels to the area-in this case Worcester County-from other areas. The Town of Ocean City estimates annual visitors to Ocean City at just over 8 million.[5] Because of the significant variability of the estimates, certain assumptions must be made. Using the 8 million visitor figure generated by the Town of Ocean City—on the assumption that the town is best capable of making such an estimate based on lodging tax receipts-one can argue that the total number of visitors to the county is higher, probably close to the 10 million figure, because some visitors to the county do not visit Ocean City. Therefore, this study uses a conservative figure of nine million as the estimate of visitors to Worcester County annually, which represents the midpoint between the Town of Ocean City estimate and the *Travel Scope* estimate.

Nature Tourism Visitors: Travel scope data also provide information on the activities visitors participate in while visiting Worcester County: 49 percent "visit beaches," 23.5 percent participate in "outdoor activities," and nine percent "visit state and national parks."[6] For the purpose of this study, it is assumed that the category titled "outdoor activities" is reasonably synonymous with nature tourism activities. Therefore, the 23.5 percent of visitors engaging in outdoor activities must be included in the estimate of nature tourism participants. Further, those who "visit state and national parks" (nine percent) represent visitors who visited Assateague Island, both the National Seashore and Assateague State Park. Since *Travel Scope* allowed for multiple responses, the nine percent of visitors who "visit state and national parks" is assumed to be already included in the overall 23.5 percent of visitors who participate in "outdoor activities," the figure used to estimate nature tourists. Thus, to arrive at an estimate of the number of visitors to Worcester County who participate in nature tourism activities, 9 million was multiplied by 23.5 percent, resulting in an estimate of 2,115,000.

An additional consideration in estimating the total number of visitors participating in nature tourism involves those who live in the county either year- around or seasonally. Based on responses to the *Worcester County Visitor Survey*, 12 percent lived in the county and an additional 6 percent owned a second home or condo in the county. Neither of these groups of county residents have been included in the estimate of nature tourism participants for the following reasons. Year–round residents of Worcester County earn their living in the county and spend money for many purposes, including recreation. However, their expenditures are different from those made by visitors to the area in that they do not represent new dollars flowing into the local economy. Therefore, expenditures by year- round residents have been excluded from the estimates presented in this study. Seasonal residents, on the other hand, earn income outside the county; therefore their spending on nature tourism should be included in the estimates. However, given the data collection methods used by this study and the existing available data from other sources, there is no practical way to estimate the portion of nature tourism spending that comes from seasonal residents of the county. Thus, for the purpose of the study, the 6 percent of the *Visitor Survey* respondents who are seasonal county residents are subsumed in the total visitor estimate presented above because of the considerable variability in total visitor estimates.

Visitor Days: To estimate the total number of visitor days, the average length of stay must be determined. To estimate the average length of stay for visitors participating in nature tourism activities, this study uses data collected as part of the *Visitor Survey* and *Travel Scope* study. The *Visitor Survey* shows that 35 percent of respondents did not spend any nights in Worcester County, while 28 percent stayed one to two nights, 25 percent stayed three to six nights, and 9 percent stayed seven to 13 nights. A small percentage stayed for extended periods ranging from 14 to 270 nights. Those who stayed overnight—and did not own property in the county—stayed an average of 4.8 nights. By comparison, *Travel Scope* estimates the average length of stay in the area is 3.1 days. While the estimate of 4.8 overnights derived from the *Visitor Survey* is assumed to be somewhat more representative of nature tourism participants in Worcester County and reflects the unique characteristics of those participating in nature tourism as compared to the typical Ocean City beach vacation, a conservative figure of 3.5 visitor days is used in this study to reflect the *Travel Scope* data.

By multiplying the average length of stay (*i.e.*, 3.5 days) times the number of visitor days (*i.e.*, 2,115,000), the number of nature tourism days are computed as 3.5 x 2,115,000=7,402,500. Another way of looking at this figure is that 7.4 million visitor days are spent annually in Worcester County by tourists engaged in nature activities.

Activity Days: The next step in estimating direct expenditures is to account for the fact that most visitors engage in more than one activity each day of their stay. For example, a visitor may in one day swim at the beach, hike, picnic, take a bike ride and camp at the state park. To develop a reasonable estimate of expenditures, one must determine how many visitors participate in each activity. The percentage of visitors engaging in each activity is referred to as the participation rate. By multiplying the participation rate by the total number of nature tourism days, the number of activity days are established, providing a basis for estimating expenditures for each activity.

Worcester County Visitors Survey and *Travel Scope* data were the primary data sources for participation rates in this study for all activities except boating (which is discussed below). Question 13 of the *Visitor Survey* provided a list of nature tourism activities and asked visitors to check the activities they planned on participating in during their visit. The survey also asked if visitors were using their own equipment or renting and whether they were participating in a tour or programme. Participation rates for each activity were then computed by dividing the number of check marks for each activity by the total number of respondents.

To estimate participation rates as conservatively as possible, only the percentage of respondents using their own equipment and not utilizing a tour or programme was used. A conservative approach is warranted because of the small sample size. For those activities for which *Travel Scope* participation rates were available, the average between the *Visitor Survey* rates and the *Travel Scope* rates was computed.

In estimating activity days for boating, this study refers to information reported in a recent study on the economic impact of the Coastal Bays conducted for the Maryland Department of Natural Resources by the Greeley-Polhemus Group, Inc. of West Chester, Pennsylvania.[7] The study estimates an average number of pleasure boating activity days for the Coastal Bays as 294,338. This figure is based on the following: (1) the number of registered boats in Worcester County (2,357) (MD DNR – Licensing and Registration Service), (2) the assumption that there are on a average 3.2 people per boat (2/2000 Maryland Coastal Bays Boating Study) and (3) boaters take an average of 32 boat trips a year (2/2000 Maryland Coastal Bays Boating Study). These boaters represent 82 percent of boaters on the bays. Thus, the calculations are as follows: number of boat licenses (2,357), multiplied by number of boat trips per year (32), multiplied by number of people per boat, divided by percentage of boaters on the bays, which equals total number of boating activity days (2,94,338).

Since 3 percent of boats observed from aerial data by Maryland DNR were canoes and kayaks, multiplying the total number of boating days by 3 percent results in 8,820 activity days for canoes and kayaks (2,94,338 × 0.03 = 8,820). According to the same survey, 82 percent were motorboats or sailboats, which results in 2,41,357 activity days (2,94,338 x 0.82).

Visitor Spending on Nature Tourism

Visitors to Worcester County create a demand for nature tourism activities that are served by the local recreation industry. Since tourism is the number one industry in the county, tourism related businesses make up a large portion of the local economy. The tourism industry includes the various types of lodging, restaurants, tour operators, specialty shop, and many other businesses that meet the needs of tourists. Many businesses that serve the year-round population, such as food, clothing and furnishing stores, realtors, banks, and others, also rely on tourists for a large portion of their business. Most tourism-dependent businesses have highly seasonal revenue with the bulk of income occurring during the May through September season. Many businesses shut down during the winter.

Visitor expenditures are challenging to estimate because there is considerable variability in the way visitors participate in a particular activity and how much they spend on the activity. It is easier, however, to establish spending estimates for some activities than for others since they require specific market transactions. For example, the cost of taking an eco tour to Assateague Island or visiting Furnace Town can be established based on the price of a ticket, but the cost of bicycling or bird-watching is more difficult to establish. Obtaining an accurate estimate of visitor spending requires an extensive survey that would be costly and time consuming to conduct. Unfortunately, no existing data source provides information on visitor expenses specific to nature tourism in Worcester County. Of some value is a survey conducted by the U.S. Department of Interior titled *National Survey of Fishing, Hunting and Wildlife-Associated Recreation*, last conducted in 1996, that provides data for Maryland. From that, values for Worcester County can be extrapolated but must then be adjusted to reflect local conditions.

To estimate visitor expenditures, this study uses published market values where appropriate and makes assumptions about visitor behaviour where no data is available. The assumptions are based on the information gathered by the *Worcester County Visitor Survey* and on expert opinion from local sources.

A major concern when estimating visitor expenses is to avoid double counting of expenditures since many purchases are not made at the time or the place where tourists actually engage in a particular activity. To avoid double counting, this study isolates food, lodging, and transportation costs and estimates them separately from the nature tourism activities themselves. The only exception are food expenditures for picnicking and camping, which are included in the daily activity values. Thus, only those expenditures directly related to a specific activity are included in the estimates.

Also, the study assumes that major purchases of equipment, gear, and clothing (*e.g.*, bicycles, kayaks, sports accessories, etc.) are typically made outside of Worcester County. While this assumption is appropriate, the spending estimates are conservative, since some tourists undoubtedly purchase some of these items in Worcester County.

TABLE 4.2

Direct Spending on Nature Tourism and Related Activities

Activity	*Participation Rate*	*Activity Days*	*Spending/Day*	*Direct Impact*
Bird-Watching	9.9%	732,848	$4.75	$3,481,026
Boating–Motor & Sail	82.0%	169,357	20.00	3,387,140
Boating–Canoe & Kayak	3.0%	8,820	35.00	308,700
Camping	9.2%	679,550	16.50	11,212,567
Fishing/Crabbing/Clamming	9.1%	673,628	7.00	4,715,393
Hiking/Biking	22.2%	1,639,654	3.25	5,328,875
Hunting/Trapping	0.9%	63,662	20.00	1,273,230
Photography–Serious	3.0%	47,746	15.00	716,190
Picnicking	27.4%	2,028,285	5.50	11,155,568
Sporting Clays	0.9%	66,623	20.00	1,332,450
Swimming	10.2%	755,055	3.50	2,642,693
Scenic/Nature Cruises	14.6%	1,077,064	10.00	10,770,638
Touring/Sightseeing	15.4%	1,139,985	3.00	3,419,955
Heritage/Historic Sites & Events	27.9%	2,065,298	4.50	9,293,839
Subtotal				$69,038,261
Food	Days	5,722,133	$10.50	$69,082,391

Lodging	Nights	2,316,983	22.00	50,973,615
Transportation	Days	2,115,000	3.50	7,402,500
Subtotal				$118,458,506
Total				187,496,767

Following are expenditures estimates for the nature tourism activities of interest to this study, followed by the estimates for food, lodging, and transportation. The amounts have been rounded; to see the actual figures, refer to Table 4.2.

Nature Tourism Activities

Bird-watching: Bird-watching has become a very popular activity that visitors pursue casually or seriously, with the interest in serious birding growing rapidly. Further, Worcester County is and important destination for serious birders, drawing visitors and tour groups from as far away as California and Arizona. Serious birders spend considerable sums on equipment, including clothing binoculars scopes, cameras, lenses, and tripods. Casual bird watchers pursue the activity without specialised equipment or gear as part of a nature hike or a boat trip. According to the *Visitor Survey,* 10 percent of bird watchers use their own equipment while 16 percent use rented equipment. Rental costs per piece of equipment range from $7 to more than $30 per day depending on the equipment. Other expenses associated with birding but usually limited to serious birders are guidebooks and other birding related souvenir items. Visitor spending is estimated to vary widely, ranging from near zero to more than $10 per activity day. Assuming that the majority of bird watchers are casual observers, a conservative daily spending estimate of $4.75 is used. Multiplied by the number of activity days (7,30,000), bird-watching results in total direct spending of $3.4 million.

Boating: Boating activities of interest to this study include motor boats (to the extent the boating activity focuses primarily on nature-based activities such as sightseeing, bird-watching, or fishing), sailboats, canoes, kayaks, and rowboats.

The *Visitor Survey* reveals that roughly half of those engaging in motor boating, canoeing, or kayaking rent their equipment while most sail boaters own their boats. While those renting equipment clearly spend money in Worcester County, those bringing their boat also spent money in the county for fuel, maintenance, and equipment. According to the Greeley-Polhemus study, the cost of renting a boat is also the most accurate equivalent to the market value of owning a boat, therefore, rental estimates are used for all categories of boating.

Motor & Sail Boats: Using the rental cost approach, Greeley-Polhemus reports average activity expenditures of $20. Adjusting the previously computed activity days for motor and sail boating for commercial rental, a new activity day total of 1,70,000 is computed, which is then multiplied by the $20 average daily expenditures for a spending estimate of $3.4 million.

Canoes and Kayaks: A representative daily rental rate of $35 for canoes and kayaks is used as the estimate of daily expenditures. Multiplying that figure by estimated number of activity days (8,820) results in a total spending estimate of $308,700.

Camping: The *Visitor Survey* indicated that 29 percent of nature tourism participants camp. Of that total, 9 percent rent their equipment. Costs associated with camping are the nightly fee for the campsite (plus the cost of admission when camping in state or national parks) and the cost of any rented equipment. Campers also frequently purchase food, household supplies, and firewood. Camping fees per person average about $8 at parks and $10 dollars at private campgrounds, for an average of $9 per activity day. Other purchases, including food, are estimated at $7.50 per day, for a total $16.50 per activity day. Multiplied by the number of activity days (6,80,000), daily expenses of $16.50 on camping generate $11.2 million in total direct spending.

Fishing/Crabbing and Clamming

Fishing, crabbing, and clamming are done from boats, the shore, piers, and docks and require bait, tackle, and gear. Data from the *Visitor Survey* indicate that of the 26 percent of nature tourists that fish, crab, and clam, 16 percent own their own equipment, while 10 percent rent equipment and gear. According to the Greeley-Polhemus study, the Maryland boating survey sets daily spending at just over $6. The value used in this study is $7 to reflect the cost of rentals. Multiplied by the number of activity days (6,70,000), daily spending of $7 on fishing, crabbing, and clamming accounts for $4.7 million.

Hiking & Bicycling: Generally speaking, bicycling is an activity pursued both very casually and with great intensity. Casual biking may be a family that brings their bicycles and makes biking a part of their Worcester County stay. Sports bicycling typically involves a lighter, high speed bicycle and specialised clothing and gear. Yet, neither form of bicycling typically involves significant expenditures aside from the initial purchase of equipment, gear, and clothing, which (as stated above) is assumed to have been made prior to the visit to Worcester County. Thus, expenditures are typically limited to on-the-way refreshments such as a bottle of water or an ice cream cone, film, and minor souvenir purchases. Also, on 7 percent of respondents to the *Visitor Survey* said that they rented equipment and less than 2 percent utilised a tour or programme, thus rental or tour costs are minimal. A conservative estimate of $2.25 to $4.25 for bicycling expenditures per activity day is used, with the average of that range at $3.25.

Spending patterns on hiking are similar to those on bicycling in that the activity is pursued both casually, with minimal special gear and clothing, and as a sport, with considerable investment in equipment, gear, and apparel. No data on the breakdown of causual versus more serious hiking exist. A daily value of $3.25 is used in this study, the same as for bicycling. By multiplying the $3.25 figure by the number of participation days for hiking and biking (1.6 million), we arrive at a total direct spending figure of $ 5.3 million.

Hunting/Trapping: The U.S. Fish and Wildlife survey reports hunting related expenditures of $25. $30 per day but those figures reflect the cost of rentals. The *Visitor Survey* data show that only 1 percent of participants rent equipment. Therefore, a conservative estimate of $20 per day is used in this study. Multiplied by 64,000 activity days, daily expenditures of $20 generate $1.3 million in total direct spending.

Photography: Photography is pursued casually by many nature visitors as part of enjoying their stay and recording their experiences, while others pursue photography as a more serious endeavour. Expenses involve the purchase of film, equipment, and the cost of rentals. The *Visitor Survey* shows that 38 percent of visitors engaged in photography to some degree, with 35 percent pursuing photography casually and 3 percent making a greater investment by renting equipment or participating in a tour or programme. Thus, it is reasonable to assume that most participation in photography is causal vacation picture taking and is included in other miscellaneous expenses (e.g., part of sightseeing or hiking). For serious photographers, daily expenses can range from $10 to $20, with an average of $15. Since it is assumed that only about three percent of participants are serious photographers, the activity days were adjusted accordingly (1,591,538 x 0.03 = 47,746). By multiplying the daily rate of $15 by the number of activity days, total direct spenuing of $716,000 is computed.

Picnicking: Picnicking involves minimal expenditures aside from food and beverages. The average cost of food and beverages for four is estimated at $20 to $24, with an average per person value of $5.50. Total direct spending of $11.2 million is computed by multiplying the daily spending rate ($5.50) by the number of activity days (2 million).

Sporting Clays: Sporting clay shooting enjoys significant popularity and is conducted at private ranges, which usually also offer a covered rifle and pistol range. Visitors select from a variety of shots that resemble waterfowl and other wildlife including ducks, geese, pheasant, doves, grouse, quail, rabbit, and fox. Visitors can purchase ammunition and rent shotguns or bring their own. The cost of targets is $10 to $30 for either 50 or 100 targets. The cost on rentals and ammunition varies. The average activity cost is estimated at $20. Multiplied by 66,600 activity days, daily spending of $20 generates total direct spending on sporting clays of $1.3 million.

Swimming: Swimming at beaches and rivers typically involves the cost of admission to state or national parks. Otherwise the cost of swimming involves the cost of renting beach chairs and an umbrella or the purchase of suntan lotion or refreshments. Swimming in pools is either included in the cost of the hotel or motel room or is done at private facilities that require a membership and are not the focus of this study. The average daily cost of swimming is estimated to be $3.50. Multiplied by 755,000 activity days, average daily spending of $3.50 generates a total of $2.6 million in direct visitor spending.

Scenic/Nature Cruises: A variety of scenic and nature cruises are offered in Worcester County featuring the coastal bays, Atlantic beaches, and the Pocomoke River. Eco-tours to Assateague Island licensed by the National Park Service cost an average of $11.50 per person. River Boat tours on the Pocomoke river cost about $8.50 per person. The average daily expenditure value is estimated at $10. Given 1.1 million activity days, average daily spending of $10 generates a total of $10.8 million in total direct spending.

Touring/Sightseeing: Touring is a form of sightseeing that may include some wildlife observation. Touring typically involves minimal expenditures for gasoline for the car and occasional small purchases such as maps, guidebooks, or souvenirs. Since touring as an activity falls outside of the transportation costs associated with the trip as a whole, the cost of gas is included in the spending estimate for this activity. An estimate of $2.50 to $3.50 per activity day is reasonable, with an average of $3 per day used in the study. Multiplied by 1.1 million activity days. $3 daily spending generates $3.4 million in total direct spending.

Visiting Historic and Heritage Sites & Events: Expenditures for this activity primarily involve the cost of admission and, depending on the museum or site, range from $4.50 to $8.50. An average activity value of $4.50 has been used. Based on 2 million activity days, this activity generates $9.3 million in direct spending.

Taken together, nature tourism activities generate a total of $69 million in direct visitor spending in Worcester County.

Food, Lodging and Transportation

As noted before, visitor spending on food, lodging, and transportation are estimated separately from expenses on nature activities to avoid double counting. Food and lodging values used in this study are based on market surveys of local prices and local expert opinion.

Food: The daily average expenditure for food is estimated at $10.50 per day per person, reflecting the fact that many groups include children and that many visitors use picnics

TABLE 4.3

Annual Direct Spending on Nature Tourism and Related Activities August 2000 through July 2001

Activity	*Direct Impact*
Bird-Watching	$3,481,026
Boating – Motor & Sail	3,387,140
Boating –Canoe & Kayak	308,700
Camping	11,212,567
Fishing/crabbing/Clamming	4,715,393
Hiking/Biking	5,328,875
Hunting/Trapping	1,273,230
Photography – Serious	716,190
Picnicking	11,155,568
Sporting Clays	1,332,450
Swimming	2,642,693
Scenic/Nature Cruises	10,770,638
Touring/Sightseeing	3,419,955
Heritage/Historic Sites & Events	9,293,839
Subtotal	$69,038,261
Food	$60,082,391
Lodging	50,973,615
Transportation	7,402,500
Subtotal	$118,458,506
Total	$187,496,707

or other informal snacks for some of their meals, while enjoying the beach, boating, hiking, or biking. Also, this estimate does not reflect the cost of food for the 23 percent of visitors who camp. For campers, the cost of food is included in the daily spending estimate for camping. By multiplying the daily rate of $10.50 by the number of activity days (5.7 million), total spending on food comes to $60.1 million.

Lodging: According to the *Visitor Survey*, 68 percent of visitors stay overnight in the area: 20 percent stay with family or friends, 33 percent camp, 26 percent stay in a hotel or mote, and 14 percent stay in a B & B. For those staying overnight, lodging costs vary considerably from $45/night for budget lodging to $120/night for luxury accommodations in historic inns and B&Bs.

Based on an informal survey of lodging costs in the county and the seasonal variability, a conservative average value of $22 per person per night is used in this study. After the number of lodging nights is computed to reflect those who do not stay overnight or do not need accommodations because they stay with family and friends or camp (which is accounted for elsewhere), a total number of 2.3 million overnights is calculated. By multiplying that number by the average per night per person cost of $22, total direct spending of $51 million is estimated.

Transportation: According to *Travel Scope*, 87 percent of visitors travel to Worcester County via automobile. But regardless of their home locations, most travel related expenses for gasoline occur outside of Worcester County. Therefore, a conservative estimate of $3.50, or about the cost of two gallons of gas, is used as the spending estimate per visitor day, or an average of $12.25 per visit, given an average length of stay of 3.5 days. Thus, the 2.1 million activity days in the county generate $7.4 million in direct visitor spending on transportation.

Added together, food, lodging, and transportation contribute another $118.5 million to the economy of Worcester Country.

Thus, nature tourism activity spending of $69 million plus $118.5 million spent on food, lodging, and transportation generate a total direct economic impact of $187.5 million on the Worcester County economy. Table 9.3 summarises the direct spending estimates.

Estimates of the Total Economic Impact of Nature Tourism

The IMPLAN Pro (Professional Social Accounting and Impact Analysis) software, developed by MIG, Inc., Stillwater, MN, was the tool used for analyzing the impact of spending by nature tourists on the economy of Worcester County. The economic data used to run the IMPLAN model was for Worcester County, extracted from the 1999 Maryland data set. Both the IMPLAN model and the Maryland data set were purchased by the University of Maryland, Institute for Governmental Service for sole use in its research projects. IMPLAN and the associated database contain a set of social/economic accounts that describe the structure of the U.S. economy in terms of transactions between households, governments, and 528 standardised industry sectors classified on the basis of the primary commodity or service produced. The database also describes that local and regional economy in terms of industry output, value added, employment, imports, and exports. A wide variety of sources are used to construct the databases, including the annual economic census conducted by the U.S. Commerce Department and the U.S. Bureau of Labour Statistics. Only those sectors of the economy relevant to Worcester County were selected and used in running the model.

The data input to the IMPLAN model are the direct expenditure estimates for nature tourism activities generated by this study. Direct expenditure estimates are based on extrapolations from the *Worcester County Visitor Survey* and *Travel Scope*.

The most powerful tools embedded in the IMPLAN model are economic multipliers. Multipliers are estimates of the extent to which direct expenditures are respent in successive waves of spending throughout the local economy. Because of the effect of economic multipliers, the total economic impact is far greater than the amount of direct spending. Since Worcester County economic data was used to run the model, the economic multipliers generated by IMPLAN are specific to Worcester County.

In general, economic multipliers are defined as the net economic change in a community or a region that results from spending attributed to a particular activity (or set of activities), even, or facility. The purpose of an economic impact analysis is to measure the economic benefits that accrue to a particular community or region.

The concept of the multiplier recognizes that changes in the level of economic activity in one area (*e.g.*, nature tourism) creates successive waves of spending throughout the economy. Nature tourists spend money on a variety of commodities related to their recreational experiences (*e.g.*, food and lodging, admissions fees, tour programmes, equipment and gear purchases or rentals, gasoline). The total amount of spending by nature tourists is the first round of spending and represents the *direct* economic impact. Direct spending estimates were presented in the previous chapter. In turn, direct sending by nature tourists stimulates economic activity as the dollars paid to the suppliers of tourism commodities (*i.e.*, hotels, B&Bs, campgrounds, restaurants, tour operators, shops) spend the money they receive as income to pay for labour (*i.e.*, salaries wages, and benefits) and supplies and to pay taxes to various levels of government. Thus, direct spending by nature tourists precipitates a second round of spending that is called the *indirect economic impact*. For example, a bed & breakfast pays wages to employees who in turn spend their household income on housing, food, consumer goods, and services. To maintain the B&B, proprietors spend money on landscape maintenance, repairs, and furnishings. The B&B also pays taxes, buys insurance, and hires the services of professionals such as a tax accountant and lawyer. Taxes are paid both to local governments, such as the county and municipality, and to the state and federal governments. Further, some money is spent to persons or businesses outside of the local area. Thus, to summarise, the suppliers of nature tourism commodities spend money in five categories:

- *Local Industry Purchases*: payments to other private sector businesses in the same jurisdiction to restock inventories, provide for future sales, maintain grounds and buildings, pay insurance premiums;
- *Direct Household Income*: payments to employees who reside in the area in the form of salaries and wages, which constitutes personal income to them;
- *Local Government Revenue*: payments to local governments for sales taxes, property taxes, or taxes on profits;
- *Nonlocal Government Revenue*: Payments to the federal and state governments for sales taxes, taxes on profits, or other taxes;
- *Non-local Leakage*: Payments to employees, shareholders, businesses, organizations, and others who reside outside the local area.

The latter two categories of spending illustrate that the local economy is part of a larger state and national economy, and some money "leaks" out of the area's economy to pay taxes or buy goods and services from entities outside the area. Only those dollars remaining in the local economy after leakage has taken place constitute the net economic gain to the area. The portion of first round expenditures that remains in the area from local inter-industry purchases, direct household income, or local government revenue is subsequently spent in one of the five ways listed above and thereby sets into motion a further round of economic activity. The portion of household income (employee wages and salaries) that is spent locally on goods and services is called the *induced* impact. The indirect and induced effects taken together are called secondary impacts. As a result of these successive waves of spending, the total economic impact of nature tourism spending is significantly larger than the initial level of direct spending. Economists call the combined effect of the successive waves of spending in an economy a *multiplier*.

Economic Impact and Employment

This study estimates direct spending by nature tourists in Worcester County to be $187.5 million, of which $69 million is spent on recreation activities and $118.5 million on food, lodging, and trip-related transportation, Care was taken not to double count expenditures and to estimate visitor expenditures conservatively. Given that level of direct spending, this study estimates an additional $50.7 million in indirect and $55.3 million in induced spending, for a total economic impact of $293.5 million. Thus, the overall economic multiplier is 1.565, which means that for every dollar of direct spending an additional 56½ cents of spending occurred in the county.

Of the $50.7 million in indirect spending, $18.1 million is attributable to recreational activities, while $32.6 million is generated by food, lodging, and transportation. The economic multiplier for indirect spending is 1.27, which means that for every dollar of direct spending, an additional 27 cents of indirect spending occurred locally. Of the $55.3 million in induced spending, $19.9 million is generated by recreational activities and $35.4 million by food lodging and transportation. The economic multiplier for induced spending is 1.295, which means that for every dollar of direct spending, an additional 29½ cents is generated in induced spending in the local economy.

Employment related to direct tourist spending is estimated to be a total of 4,611 full-time equivalent jobs in Worcester County. Actual jobs may be considerably more, since many tourism-related jobs are part time or seasonal. The total number of jobs created by tourism spending—including those generated by indirect and induced spending—is 6,927 full-time equivalents. In summary, $187.5 million in direct spending by visitors on nature tourism and related activities and on food, lodging, and transportation in Worcester County is estimated to create a total economic impact of $293.5 million, with 6,927 full-time equivalent jobs created.

Then, using an economic input-output model, one can estimate the total impact of nature tourism on the economy, which is greater than direct spending by visitors due to the effect of economic multipliers (i.e., re-spending in the local economy), and includes indirect and induced effects. The indirect impact is the re-spending of dollars in the local economy on wages to employees, operating expenses, taxes, etc. The induced impact is the portion of employee wages and salaries that is spent locally on goods and services. Taken together, direct indirect, and induced impacts are the total economic impact, which provides the basis for estimating the number of jobs supported by nature tourism. To collect information on nature tourism visitors, the authors of this study conducted a year-long survey in various locations throughout the county from August 2000 through July 2001. One thousand two hundred seventy-nine visitors completed a short survey that asked about a dozen questions about their visit, including where they were from, how long and where they were staying and in which activities they participated. Visitors were not asked directly about their spending since such questions are generally considered intrusive. The data collected from the survey was used in the economic analysis, but beyond that, represents a valuable resource for local officials and members of the business community wanting information on the characteristics of visitors to the area.

Using information from the visitor survey and other data sources, this study estimates annual direct visitor spending on nature tourism and cultural activities of $69 million plus an additional $118 million for food, lodging, and transportation, for a total of $187 million in direct spending.

Using the IMPLAN input-output model, this study estimates the total economic impact of nature tourism on the county's economy. Given the $187 million in direct spending, this study estimates an additional $50 million in indirect and $55 million in induced spending, for a total economic impact of $293 million. The overall economic multiplier is 1.565, which means that for every dollar of direct spending an additional 56½ cents of spending occurred in the county. Employment related to direct tourist spending is estimated to be a total of 4,611 full-time equivalent jobs in Worcester County. Actual jobs may be considerably more, since many tourism-related jobs are part time or seasonal.

Sustainable Design and Ecolodges

Over the past few years, several documents have emerged that analyse the development of ecolodges and ecotourism facilities on the basis of principles of sustainability. However, there appears to be some confusion on the scale and magnitude of development of such areas according to Epler Wood, who reports that ecotourism continues to be misunderstood in resort advertising schemes, while the term 'ecoresort' has yet to be appropriately defined (Shundich 1996). For instance, a tourism industry trade publication recently wrote that 'Another recent and perhaps surprising region for ecoresort development is India...There is interest in genuine cultural experiences within the country. One man has proposed a historical tour of India by rail.'

Interest in sustainable ecotourism design took flight in the early 1990s in part as a result of a US national park service publication dedicated to the principles of sustainable design. Two events took place in the United States that prompted the development of this book. The first was the National Park Service Vail Symposium in October 1991 which discussed, among other things, the severity of environmental stresses within parks; while the second was the Virgin Islands National Park initiative in November 1991, which specifically dealt with issues related to sustainable design in parks and protected areas (US Department of the Interior 1993). The latter publication explores interpretation, natural and cultural resources, site design, building design, energy management, water supply waste prevention, and facility and maintenance operations in its overview of sustainable design. Of particular importance is its extensive checklist for sustainable building design that emphasises and respects the many inter relationships of all parts of the natural and cultural aspects of the site. However, these were not the first attempts to integrate the developments of humankind with the natural world (especilly parks), as evident in the seminal work of Miller (1976, 1989) on ecodevelopment.

Although the US Department of the Interior book is devoted to facility design and construction in *parks*, there is a more generic section that deals specifically with sustainable tourism development. Here the authors advocate using the principles of Aesculapia, which is the Greek place of healing. From this perspective, 'nature is respected for its restorative qualities. The human experience is set in harmony with the environment, and an opportunity is created to allow a reconnection of human need to the natural systems on which all life is based' (US department of the interior 1993: 58). This type of design principles would then strive to meet the following criteria, according to the authors:

1. provide education for visitors on wildlife, native

cultural resources, historic features, or natural features;

2. involve indigenous populations in operations and interpretation to foster local pride and visitor exposure to traditional values and techniques;
3. accomplish environmental restoration;
4. provide research and development on, and/or demonstration projects of, ways to minimize human impacts on the environment;
5. provide spiritual or emotional recuperation;
6. provide relaxation and recreation; and
7. educate visitors to realise that knowledge of our local and global environment is valuable and will empower their ability to make informed decisions.

Russell et al. (1995: x) define an ecolodge as 'a nature-dependent tourist lodge that meets the philosophy and principles of ecotourism'. Although they underscore the importance of the ecolodge concept from an educational and experiential perspective, they suggest that it is the philosophical tie with ecological sensitivity that must defined these operations. The importance of ecology is also underscored by the Ecotourism Society, which feels that such lodges promote an educational and participatory experience while at the same time being developed and managed in regard to the local environment in which it exists (Epler Wood in Shundich 1996). Russell *et al.* distinguish between traditional lodges and ecolodges using the 12 points. They further distinguish between the ecolodge and the nature-based lodge, with the latter being associated with fishing, skiing, and luxury retreats.

The philosophical issues related to ecolodges identified above is one considered by Anderson (1993, 1994), who feels that along with environmental codes of ethics, a low-impact approach to the design of ecotourism facilities needs to be employed for such facilities to be truly sustainable—an approach that he suggests would entail a complete reworking of the conventional design of architects. Anderson's work is well publicised in the field of ecotourism, especially his advocacy of a number of principles which broadly defined, include organisational issues (e.g. has an analysis been done of the area' ecological sensitivity?), site planning issues (e.g. minimise trail crossing points at rivers and streams), building design issues (e.g., maintenance of the ecosystem should take priority over view or dramatic design statements), energy resource and utility infrastructure issues (e.g. consider the use of passive or active solar or wind energy sources wherever practical), waste management issues (e.g. provide facilities for recycling), and evaluation (e.g. whether accommodation is made for older guests and physically disabled individuals). Andersen has been able to operationalise many of these design features in his Lapa Rios Resort development on the Osa Peninsula of Costa Rica's Pacific coast. This development has a main lodge in addition to 14 private bungalows which were built by local engineers with the removal of only one tree. (See also Hadley and Crow, 1995, Gurung, 1995, and Wight, 1995 for good discussions on the guidelines and requirements for the design of ecotourism facilities).

Given the low-capacity and low-impact philosophies of ecotourism development, a logical question is: at what scale does the ecolodge model *not* apply? That is, when is a development considered too big? This question, at least peripherally, has been addressed by Ayala (1996). As an international ecoresort developer, she believes both that ecotourism is becoming a segment of mass tourism, and that it is not incompatible with beach tourism. She supports this view by suggesting that there is the need to diversify the vast number of sea, sun, and sand products through the addition to ecotourism (but not at the exclusion of other hard-path experiences). Ayala feels that the line between ecotourists and conventional tourists is least detectable in long-haul travel, citing similarities in their levels of education, household income, and their occupations. In resting is the fact that (1) that ability to travel long distances is directly related to one's wealth and, (2) wealth is directly related to education and occupation. Ayala fails to discuss other factors (e.g. psychograhics) that determine differences in travel types. For example, the assumption being made is either that all long-haul tourists are ecotourists; or that all ecotourists are simply long-haul traveler. Ayala further writes that many of the mega-resort chains in Africa and Central America go so far as to donate money to conservation efforts. However, if the link is being made to ecotourism, which is the focus of her article, then one wonders what percentage of the revenue from the hotels stays within the local communities and what percentage flows back to North America or Europe. Could such an initiative by the big companies be an appeasement mechanism or marketing scheme designed to look green? (See also the work of Thomlinson and Getz (1996) on scale ecotourism development.

It is not easy being sceptical about published work in this area, but increasingly scepticism is what is needed to address some of the issues related to the philosophy and implementation of ecotourism, especially as they relate to ecoresorts. Will ecotourism's fall from grace be directly attributable to the belief and practice that it fits very nicely as a form of mass tourism, and that mega-ecotourists are the solution to bring ecotourism to the masses? Is this the rationale for their development—the intrinsic need to not deny the masses their place in the sun (or rather rainforest)? Or rather is it simply that from an extrinsic motivational perspective, it is big business making money the old-fashioned way? Having seen some of these developments first hand, one merely has to dig a bit more closely at some of the unsustainable features of the development. For example, an ecolodge in Mexico recently developed by a large international company used grass and other materials not indigenous to the area in the design of the facility. In addition, no interpretive programmes had been developed to enable tourists to learn about or experience the natural and cultural attractions of the area. Such developments are merely cosmetic, often with few educational and sustainable features, which presumably are important to this segment, and undermine what Hawkins (1994) and others have suggested about ecotourism as being minimum density and low impact.

Ecolodge Research

Ecolourism and the ecolodge concept have been misused by resort advertisers in the past. For this reason research needs to play a stronger role in providing leadership in this area. The following few examples serve to illustrate some of what exists in the area of ecolodge research.

Russell *et al.* (1995) undertook an international ecolodges survey of 28 operators in nine regions around the world (Belize, Costa Rica, Peru, Brazil, Ecuador, the state of Alaska, Australia, New Zealand, and Africa). This study discovered that many of the lodges were fund in or adjacent to protected areas, with outstanding natural beauty acting as a key to success of the operation. Most of the ecolodges sampled were small in size, accommodating about 24 gusts, with some successful operations in Amazonia catering up to 100 guests. Prices for accommodation (single night) meals, and local transportation were approximately US$130-170. The authors felt that although most of the ownership had been typically small scale and independent, corporate ownership was becoming more common. They cited the P&O line in Australia and the Hilton in Kenya as two examples of this recent phenomenon. Finally, they suggested that very few such lodges exist in North America owing to the existing reliance on camping and other, more comfortable recreational lodges. This finding is supported in a recent market study of ecotourism in Alberta and British Columbia (ARA Consultants 1994). However, according to Wight (1995), this is not necessarily what is happening. She feels that market research does not indicate that such a trend is due to market research does not indicate that such a trend is due to market preference, but rather it is due to the demand for a range of accommodation. To Wight, a better question would be to ascertain the range of accommodation types supplied by the region or destination area, where, she feels, there is an abundance of the conventional hotel/motel opportunities. She does, however, feel that there is a distinct lack of adventure-type, small-scale, fixed-roof accommodation.

The hard aspects of ecotourism can be identified, at least in part, by non-permanent types of dwellings, including tents and hammocks. The ecotourism experience grows continually softer through fixed-roof units (cabins and lodges) on-site, and through fixed-roof dwelling off-site, usually in the form of hostels, hotels, and resorts. This hard-soft accommodation continuum relates in part to the work of Laarman and Durst (1987), at least in part, who suggested that one of the hard and soft dimensions of ecotourism was the physical rigour of the trip. Those who were prepared to walk extensively in back-country regions, sleep in camps or crude shelters, or tolerate poorer sanitary conditions were said to have been interested in more of a hard-path ecotourism experiences.

If this continuum is to apply to North America, it is logical to ask whether or not such operations are applicable to consumptive or non-consumptive forms of recreation. This issue has not been adequately addressed in the literature, at least from the Canadian perspective, and is an issue that is of the utmost importance as outfitters and operators wrestle with how to refit their enterprises to accommodate the changing recreational focus in the north, because, as

Anderson/Fast (1996a: 5—4) suggest, 'depending on the characteristics of the package and the participating tourists, outfitter camps [the only form of accommodation in many remote regions of Canada's north] may or may not be appropriate.'

Finally, literature on ecoresorts seems to indicate that accommodation, although important, is not the overriding motivation for visiting regions. ARA (1994), for example, places accommodation below the natural setting and wildlife viewing (of primary importance), and other secondary activities related to the experience. To this, Wight (1995) adds supported by suggesting that accommodation is an enabler of the overall ecotourism experience; basically tourists select the experience, then choose the accommodation. Often, though, prearranged package tours dictate much of the on-site experience, including choice of accommodation, restricting the opportunity for ecotourists to choose lodging, and reinforcing the point that there is an element of ambiguity as to just what ecotourism entails. According to Grenier *et al.* (1993: 9), 'one persc .'s ecotourism dream may be another's touristic nightmere.'

One of the unfortunate realities of ecotourism is that despite its altruistic intentions, to date there is little evidence that it is less intrusive than other types of tourism development. It is indeed frustrating that we continue to talk of appropriate means by which to control development, yet have very few successes to report on. Those who do report success have perhaps not been operating long enough to let, for instance, the destination life cycle unfold. In many localities around the world, local initiatives are chipping away at the conditions or circumstances that continue to plague ecotourism development. It is within the local areana that such change must occur.

CHAPTER FIVE

Potential Development of National Parks in Indonesia

National park has more than woods to offer to the community. It has its own future plan for the next generation if taken care properly. The resources that can be listed are endless. This chapter will discuss the threats that are faced by stand potential development that can be implemented on the national parks. Due to some constraints over gathering resources and availability of information, this paper will focus or eon Tanjung Puting National Park. However, some of the more general issues will apply to most, if not all national parks of Indonesia. The threats on the national pars are many, but there is one common piece that will relate to most of them, that is illegal logging. What really is illegal logging and how it does occur will be discussed on this chapter. In a country like Indonesia, nothing gets solved easily. Even if you have a system of law and regulation, but the culture and the societies has the stronger force. The country and the world represented by the UN and other stakeholders know what the core of the problem is and how they should deal with it, but the reality seems to fight against it.

The construction of political system mixed with the

cultures and national values make the solution just so difficult to accomplish. Only by striving effort from all levels and dimensions of different parties will the problems be solved if not at let reduced.

Ecotourism and National Parks

It is no doubt that ecotourism relies strongly to the existence of national parks. Potential for ecotourism development in Indonesia mainly lies in its resources. Indonesia is known as country with mega-diversity, in terms of biodiversity, Indonesia is home for 10% of flowered flora in the world; 12% of mammals, 16% of amphibia, and reptiles, 17% of birds, 25% of fish and 15% of insects (World Tourism Organisation, nd.). So, it is quite obvious that a national park is one of the main resources for ecotourism development in Indonesia. Although it has a vague and no universal definition across many different cultures, most people will agree to associate ecotourism with environment. According to World Tourism Organisation (n.d). So, it is quite obvious that a national park is one of the main resources for ecotourism development in Indonesia. Although it has a vague and no universal definition across many different cultures, most people will agree to associate ecotourism with environment. According to World Tourism Organisation (n.d.) ecotourism Indonesia is seen as a model for the integration of tourism and conservation purposes, a model for cot efficient development during the difficult time, a model for public as well as tourist educational means for being responsible to the environment and cultural heritage, a model for community empowerment, which all are indicators for sustainable development.

Among all the national parks in Indonesia the type of national park that will be discussed on this paper is the forest. Over a hundred million of forest areas in Indonesia are also a potential indicator, 30 million hectares of which are protected forest, and over 15 million hectares are nature preservation area comprises of national parks, grand forest parks and nature recreation parks (World Tourism Organisation, n.d.). Tanjung Puting just like any other national parks in Indonesia share many commonalities such as the biodiversity, historical values, natural wonders and many other beautiful existences. But there is one thing that makes Tanjung Puting stand out among the rest, which is the orang utan. Many people recognize and visit the tanjung Puting National Park because of its orang utan. The Parks' main tourist attractions have been centrered around the orng utan rehabilitation centre and the scenic river cruises on the Sekonyer River for a long time (Susilo, 1997).

The Threats and Potential Development

The class presentation for this paper was started by asking a question to the audience about what they would see when visiting national park. The answers suggested that there was no initial knowledge regarding the unpleasant occurrences and scenes that may happen in a national park. As a costumer, a person will usually acquire the fine image about the product, but as an expert, the image is rather more complex as a result from analysis of different perspectives and resources. That's what this paper is based on, that the resources and information were obtained from the subject matter expert. An interview with Mr. Mawardi was conducted on October 12, 2002 in addition to the literature findings. Mr. Mawardi is the former inspector general of Ministry of Forestry and Estate Crops of Indonesia. According to Mawardi (personal communication, October 12, 2002) some of the threats that has been identified in the national parks in Indonesia are illegal logging, forest conversion; roads building, forest fire, reef destruction, mining and poaching. Out of all those threats, nothing has reached the media and the world attention more than the illegal logging problem. And that's what will be discussed further on this paper.

As stated previously the introduction that these problems are not easy to solve because of the complexity of system components along with the stakeholders who are involved in it. Those that pay the most can buy their way in so the only way to conserve forests in Indonesia maybe to bribe whoever happens to be in control locally, more than the loggers, poachers and miners, or to subsidize dangerous military operations (Ecological anarchy, n.d.). The worst part is that the influential party in the country keeps using the rule just to become stronger and even more powerful using any force necessary. One perfect example would be the man by the name of Abdul Rasyid. According to Environmental Investigation Agency as reported by Four Corners, The Tiber mafia (n.d.) in 1999 they first exposed how a company owned by a timer bron called Abdul Rsyid were openly logging within a world famous National Park, Tanjung Putting. Abdul Rasyid is now a member of the MPR – Indonesia's highest Parliamentary body.

Figure 1 describes the system components involved in the illegal logging problem. The system components are interrelated to the stakeholders of the illegal logging of the national pars directly and indirectly. The stakeholders are:

- Timber barons
- Consuming countries
- Government of Indonesia (GOI)
  - Ministry of Forestry and Estate Crops (MoFEC)
  - Ministry of tourism and Culture
- Local community
- Non-Environmental Organisation (NGO)
  - Environmental Investigation Agency (EIA)
  - Telapak Indonesia

- The environmentalist
- The "investors"
- The tourism operators and tourists
- The media

According to Badan Pengendalian Dampak Lingkungan, Serba-serbi (2000) one of the main factors of the illegal logging is the timber deficit faced by the producer/supplier that forces them to satisfy the needs through uncontrolled logging and illegal trading. There is a specific type of wood that people are after for because of its fine quality and the rareness. Four Corners, The Timer mafia (n.d.) stated that Environmental Investigation Agency found that the main timber species being exploited in the park for the global markets is ramin (Gonystylus spp.) a tropical hardwood that grows in peast swamp and the lowland fresh water swamp forests in Boneo, Sumatra and peninsula Malaysia.

In spite of what's being exploited, a report by E.O. Colijn as cited from German Primte Centrer (n.d.) argues that after the falloff the Suharto government in 1998 several groups with different motives started to invade the protected areas. One of the groups comprises that local people who felt betrayed by the central government that for 33 years had been taking advantage of their natural resources and/or had forcedly displaced them from established conservation areas. A second group is formed by poor people who, paid by other groups like forest and palm oil concessionaires, sawmill owners and even local leaders, encroached protected areas. Finall there are the thus, called 'oknum' in Indonesia, who just grab whatever they can lay their hand son. Corrupt military and officials are protecting all those involved.

There are many things that need to be improved in Tanjung Puting as well as other national parks in Indonesia. When asked what the key components would be a potential development towards national parks in Indonesia, Mawardi (personal communication, October 12, 2002) replied that there should be an inventory system in place and promotion towards the existing tourism potential and increase in security over management of the national parks, and reinvestment of ecotourism revenue towards a sustainable development and preservation of the national pars. Simple message goes a long way as a means to educate people about caring for the environment. Some of the things that Tanjung Puting can offer according to Susilo (1997) are the orng utan rehabilitation centrer, the proboscis monkey, scenic river cruises, bird watch (storm's stork), wildlife flower (black orchid) and a walk in the jungle.

There seems to be some strong common thoughts between the stakeholders regarding solutions to the illegal logging problem in Tanjung Puting National Park. Author's initial response as to what would be the best possible solution after learning about the issue is to enforce the law and regulations. These tasks are easy ride obviously. However, E.O. Golikn as cited from German Primate Center (n.d.) stated that while law-enforcement should definitely be improved, it is only part of the solution. It will prove to be a very difficult, if not impossible, task to solve the illegal logging problem in Indonesia without simultaneously addressing the timber deficit, corruption inside MoFEC and improvement of the situation of poor farmers in Indonesia. Dealing with the powerful and greedy individuals involves a great life endangerment. Mawardi (personal communication, October 12, 2002) agreed that in order to solve the problem, there needs to be an increase in cooperation between the national park management with the foreign stakeholders and digging out the international funds in a form of compensation for the preservation of "the lung of the world". The Environment Investigation agency and Telapak Indonesia went on to be more specific over the recommendation towards the solution of the illegal logging issue in Tanjung Puting. As posted by Four Corners, The Timber Mafia (n.d.), EIA and Telapak Indonesia affirmed that governments need to develop new procurement policies that demonstrate timber and wood products have come from legal sources, industry needs to adopt transparent chain of custody processes which allows timber tracking from source to market. Producing countries need to formalize a system of cross border cooperation between national enforcement authorities, and to enact legislation allowing the confiscation of illegal timber and those dealing in it outside the country o origin. No single action will end this trade and we all have to accept our own responsibility.

National Park: Tourism Marketing Strategy

Tourism Marketing strategy are the National Park Board & Authority staff, elected representatives and decision makers throughout the Park, and all stakeholders who may be directly affected and have a role to play in its implementation. This is a dynamic document which will be reviewed and updated taking into accqunt changes in the national tourism structure, developments on sustainable tourism, and as a result of increased knowledge from market research. The Cairngorms National Park was established in March 2003 by the Scottish Parliament, and assumed its operational powers on September 1. It encompasses 1,467 sq miles, and is the UK's largest National Park. Geographically its stretches from Grantown on Spey in the west to the Angus Glens in the east, from Ballater in the north to Dalwhinnie in the south.

The stakeholders within the Cairngorms National Park both epitomize its diversity, and the opportunities offered by collaboration throughout the Park. In order to assist the National Park Authority in effectively developing, promoting and marketing the areas, the Tourism Development Working Group was established, by the Park Authority, to bring together various interests and drive forward positive developments and improvements in tourism in the area.

The Group comprises representatives from a wide range of key organizations, including the current three area tourist boards, Visit Scotland, representatives from local tourism businesses and commercial concerns, environmental organizations, government agencies, local authorities and community groups, each with an interest in tourism and an influence in the future of the Park. A full list of stakeholders and their respective roles in tourism is at Appendix 1.

The Tourism Vision for the Future

The vision for the future of tourism in the area is to:

Establish the Cairngorms as one of the most spectacular National Parks in the world with a reputation for superb visitor facilities and services, and access to a landscape of unrivalled natural beauty in which businesses can flourish in harmony with the natural environment.

Overall Objective of the Tourism Marketing Strategy

"To develop a world class brand and marketing strategy which contributes to the sustainable year round economic prosperity of the area, for the benefit of all those who live, work and enjoy the real, primarily through the attraction of visitors who recognize the quality of the natural environment and the incredible diversity of the product – the Cairngorms National Park"

Key Aims of the strategy

Sustainable tourism is the overarching framework for tourism in the Cairongorms, which the Park Authority is striving to develop and improve further. The Tourism Marketing Strategy is set within this context, with the key aims of the strategy being to:

- Utilise the opportunities created by the designation of the cairngorms as a National Park to position the area as a quality destination for all to enjoy.

- Encourage both new and returning visitors to continue returning to the area, throughout the year either on a more frequent or longer stay basis.
- Ensure that all marketing activity is delivered in an integrated and co-ordinated way, thereby maximizing the area's potential.

All of which will take due regard of the four main aims of the cairngorms National Park, namely:

- To conserve and enhance the natural and cultural heritage;
- To promote the sustainable use of the natural resources of the area;
- To promote understanding and enjoyment (including enjoyment in the form of recreation) of the special qualities of the area by the pubic;
- To promote sustainable, social and economic development of the communities of the area.

Strategic & Policy Context

The Tourism Marketing Strategy has been prepared taking cognizance of the fact that there are other marketing and development agendas to be taken into consideration, not least Visit Scotland and the three Area Tourist Boards, and they have a direct or indirect influence on the viability and success of initiatives proposed.

The European charter for Sustainable Tourism seeks to balance a market led approach to development and marketing activity, within designated protected regions cross Europe, such as the Cairngorms, with the need to enhance the quality of life of those who live, work and spend their leisure time there, and the conservation and enhancement of the natural and cultural heritage of the region. The sustainable tourism approach means seeking harmony between economic, environmental and social aims.

In National Parks and other protected areas, sustainable development programmes demonstrate the desire to promote economic development.

The Cairngorms National Park is currently pursuing the adoption of the Charter, which will require stakeholders to develop a greater understanding of sustainable development as a tool for economic growth. The process of developing and implementing the Charter will provide stakeholders in the Park with this understanding.

The UK Tourism Structure

As the UK appointed former British Tourist authority, Visit Britain has a remit to promote Britain to an international audience. The cairngorms National Park is included within the product portfolio of Britain's National Park's Visit Britain are currently considering, in conjunction with the Association of national Park Authorities (ANAPA) how best to effectively market all of the UK's National Parks and the Cairngorms will be kept up to date on developments.

Visit Scotland exists to support the development of the tourism industry in Scotland and to market the country as a quality destination. As one of two National Parks in Scotland, the Cairngorms National Park is part of the Visit Scotland portfolio both as and destination in its own right and through the promotion of tourism businesses within the Park. The organization has a direct involvement in marketing the Park.

Local Area Structure

Currently there are three area tourist boards directly involved in the promotion of tourism within the park. These are Aberdeen and Grampian Tourism Board (AGTB). Angus & Dundee Tourist Board (ADTB), Highlands of Scotland Tourist Board (HOST). This will change in April 2005, with the ATB structure replaced in the Cairngorms area by three hubs of Visit Scotland.

In establishing the Tourism Development Working Group, the National Park Authority has drawn together representatives from all aspects of the tourism industry to work together for the collective benefit of the area as a whole.

The Tourism Market - Key Issues

Scottish Tourism Market

Market research (available on www.scotexchane.net) has highlighted potential opportunities for the Cairngorms in attracting identified national niche markets to the area. These include recreational niche markets such as walking, cycling, skiing & field sports, other activity based holiday markets, and the short breaks market.

Prediction of future trends suggests that Scotland's visitor profile will continue to mature, but will become more educated and affluent. They are increasingly active, well traveled and have high expectations of customer service and value for money. In depth analysis of future trends is at Appendix 10.

The Cairngorms Tourism Market

The interim results of the Cairngorms Visitor Survey (2003-2004) provides the most up to date information on visitors to the Park as a whole, where they come from and why they come to the area.

There are a high number of visitors who return to the Cairngorms on a regular basis 80% of visitors are form the UK, 48% of whom are from Scotland, with the main visitor group being two adults on holiday. Overseas visitors account for the remaining 20%. The percentages and origins of these visitors varies throughout the Park area.

Currently three Area Tourist Boards seek to attract

visitors to their respective areas within the Cairngorms National Park as part of marketing efforts. Information on the number of visitors, the number of bed nights and the visitor spend for each area as a whole shows that tourism in each area is of significant economic value to the area These three areas receive 5.3 million tourist trips, 20.3 million bed nights and a visitor spend of £1,054 million. There is a need for this information to be available specifically for the National Park area, and work is required to deliver this information. More information per ATB area is at Appendix 12.

Quality Service

Dramatic mountain scenery, diverse wildlife, engaging heritage and culture, and an array of excellent amenities set a standard, but they do not set apart a destination in the modern market place. For the visitor to choose, there is a need to offer a unique overall experience. This sits well with the sophisticated modern visitor, seeking to enjoy maximum benefit from minimum preparation. It is providing this level of world class service that will set the Park apart within the global market place. There is a need to ensure that the quality of service throughout the Park in all aspects of tourism matches the quality of the environment.

The Competing Market Place

There are significant changes in the market:

- Competition is in a global market place and as such there is a need to provide differentiated information, to make it easy for the customer to book and to provide world-class service at the destination.
- The increasing competition in the marketplace together with the increasing sophistication of consumers is resulting in complex tourism products. Collaboration between private firms and private and public organizations enhance the ability to develop and

promote such products.

- The demand for visitors looking for 'new experiences' is growing.
- Repeat customers and friends and relatives being advised to come provide the largest source of visitors.

Competitors

With ever-greater ease of travel, visitors continue to broaden their horizons. The tourism market is no longer confined to national boundaries. The Cairngorms National Park is competing in a global market place, where attraction is judged against the rest of the world. Though the Park has many exemplary qualities. Its attributes are matched or exceeded, in some other accessible part of the world Amenity therefore will no longer be enough to guarantee visitors.

Research shows that the competitive edge is maintained by placing significant emphasis on enhancing the overall experience of the tourist. The Cairngorms main competitors are potential experience of the tourist. The Cairngorms main competitors are potentially identified as other scenic, iconic parts of Scotland such as Loch Ness & Skye, Other UK national Parks in particular Luch Lomond & the Trossachs; activity based holiday throughout the UK (with particular attention to marketing activity in the Fort William area), and in an international context, Ireland and Wales as tourism destinations. A breakdown of competitor analysis is at appendix 6.

Year Round Destination

Geographically, the attraction of the Cairngorms National Park is diverse. The mountainous west gives way to the valley glends of the south, and the flatter, rural landscapes of the east and north. The resulting visitor profile is greatly influenced by this diversity, but is also significantly shaped by the seasonable profile.

Visitor numbers peak in the summer. Winter sports enthusiasists boost visitor numbers in the mountain areas around the Cairngors Massif, including the three ski areas in the Park. Leisure walkers tend to prefer the longer days of late spring, summer and into early autumn, with the Angus Glenspopular at these times of year. Unsurprisingly, family visits follow a pattern reflected by the school holiday calendar. Mature couples, those taking weekend breaks and overseas visitors might be expected in relatively consistent numbers throughout the whole of the recognised tourist season.

The Cairngorms has the ability to be a year round location and the lengthening of the season to encourage visitors in the shoulder months is a key issue for the Tourism Marketing Strategy to address.

Products of the Park

The Tourism marketing Strategy seeks to add value to products and services that are special to the Park, by establishing and promoting the image of the Park and encouraging partnerships within the Park. By working together, producers, distributors and retailers can add value by guaranteering a range of products and foodstuffs as originating from the Park, perhaps with breeding or harvesting in traditional ways to further differentiate and emphasize the quality. A selection of produce already exists which with support would be suitable candidates to brand as 'Produce of the Park'.

SWOT Analysis

The results of the SWOT analysis of the Park as a tourist destination provides key indicators for the delivery of the key aims of the Strategy.

Strengths

- An outstanding natural clean fresh environment,

with natural beauty and open spaces National Park designation

- Diverse range of year round outdoor activities which can be easily accessed
- Wildlife in its natural environment
- Large cluster of varied visitor attractions
- Highland Games
- Royal Deeside

Weaknesses

- Lack of integrated visitor information that is available and the information that is needed
- Variable standards of quality and service
- Lack of wet whether facilities
- Poor public transport infrastructure in and around, and to the Park Shortage of evening entertainment &early closing of catering outlets Lack of staff accommodation.

Opportunities

- Redevelopment of Aviemore
- Develop & encourage quality standards for the Park to improve visitors experience
- Develop the cairngorms National Park Brand as a strong brand Develop co-ordination and collaborative thinking to develop information on inclusive accommodation / activity packages and market them.
- Develop the tourism potential of the area's cultural heritage improve integrated information & interpretation provision Capitalise on the growth in interest in the environment
- Develop tourism best practice, drawing on experiences elsewhere

- Improve the environmental performance of businesses and market this aspect.

Threats

- No effective collaboration
- Potential environmental damage due to inadequate management
- Climate Change
- Erosion of political support for National Park principles
- Inadequate funding.

Delivery of the Key Aims

The Tourism Development Working Group will lead the implementation of the Tourism marketing Strategy, forming a variety of sub groups as necessary, with the National Park Authority acting as co-ordinator of all activity. All of these aims will only be effectively delivered through a collaborative approach, with all stakeholders working with the National Park Authority to ensure its successful implementation.

Branding

Develop a strong brand for the Cairngorms that presents a coherent image to visitors and contributes to the economic prosperity of the area.

A Brand identity must be agreed and developed, consistent with customer trends. The elements and temperament of the Brand building campaign must be defined and a launch programme for the Brand agreed. The Cairngorms Brand will seek to provide a cohesive image for the area as a whole within which existing and potentially new strong brands will continue to develop and evolve.

Communications: Consumer

Utilise the opportunities created by the designation of

the Cairngorms National Park to position the area as an attractive destination to visit.

With ever increasingly expectations by the visiting public, the region must be seen to move with the times' and provide a modern and sophisticated experience.

Make all visitors aware that they are in a National Park and engage visitors in caring for the national Park through appreciation and understanding of the indigenous nature, heritage and culture.

Routes cross the National Park, so many people therefore will 'visit' the Park without necessarily realizing so. The creation of a sense of arrival at entry points, such as railway stations, roadside service stations and significant settlements in the Park, is important. The values of the Park must be communicated in clear, concise terms. The use of interpretation will seek to further strengthen the bond between the geography and the designation of the Park.

Communications; Stakeholders

Create a communications plan to engage with key personnel to inform and communicate information relating to the National Pak and raise awareness of the Park's brand values the new brand image and opportunities to use it.

There is need for coherent advice and information for Park visitors. Communicating this information and encouraging pan park familiarization is a key factor in strengthening relationships with the park area.

The resources devoted to developing both the brand and the marketing plan will be best utilized if they are introduced both to the business and wider community and the identified target markets. Communications will form a key part of the Action Plan.

Market Research

Undertake comprehensive market research, to understand customer expectations and indictors for future development.

Customers of the Park are likely to have diverse wants and needs. In depth information therefore needs to be gathered to understand, meet, and hopefully exceed these expectations. Analyzing customer feedback, balanced with information on future trends will ensure that the customer is better understood and future marketing initiatives can be tailored accordingly.

Product Development

Encourage, develop and promote opportunities, new product development and services that meet customer needs and which are consistent with Park heritage and environmental values.

The sustainable development of market led product development should be encouraged and supported throughout the Park.

Quality Service standards Provide visitors with a world class experience which competes within the worldwide market place and which encourages return visits and recommendations to friends and relatives.

Numerous surveys show that word of mouth recommendation carries the highest level of trust in potential visitors. The emerging culture needs to be one that values individual visitors as a potential lead to the next. Customer care is vital therefore in encouraging both repeat and new tourism activity in the area and initiatives aimed at developing and improving the quality of service throughout the Park should be supported.

Partnership Approach

Collaboration throughout the Park, on marketing

initiatives, information sharing and mutual resolutions to shared concerns.

Existing initiatives are developing which foster cooperation within the Park area. These should be enabled to continue to develop. The Tourism development Working Group broadly represents all sectors of the industry, within the Park area, and provides a basis for discussion & development. The Cairngorms Chamber of Commerce offers a representative forum for any commercial concern located in the Park boundary. Out with the ark boundary, there is a need to engage with national organisations and initiatives to ensure effective collaboration opportunities are maximized.

Monitoring Success

Appropriate indictors and targets will be developed against individual programmes and initiatives within the Tourism Marketing strategy Action Plan. The overall performance of the strategy will be monitored as part of the Sustainable tourism Strategy and Action Plan.

It is important to note that these specific aims, whilst being integral to National Park's marketing effort, actually have broader tourism development implications. They will be central themes within the Park's Sustainable Tourism Strategy and Action Plan, being developed as part of the process of attaining the European Charter for Sustainable Tourism.

CHAPTER SIX

Sustainable Tourism in Protected Areas: Prospectus for Action for Scotland's National Parks

It goes on to identity the current sustainable tourism structures and activities in each Park area and how these might be strengthened in order to meet the requirements of the Charter. The charter is about reognising parks which follow the right approach in developing and management sustainable tourism, it does not seek to measure the absolute qualities of the park in terms of landscape and facilities.

The charter falls into three separate parts:

- For the parks themselves;
- For tourism businesses in the parks; ad,
- For tour operators bringing visitors into the pars.

To date only the first part has been developed by Europarc, and 13 Parks have been awarded Charter status on this basis.

The Relevance of the Charter to Scotland's Parks

Whilst tourism is an extremely important activity in both Parks and Critical to the local economies neither National Park has a strategy for sustainable tourism. The Charter provides an opportunity for the Parks to align developing tourism policy and action to current international thinking and practice, and as new parks developing sustainable tourism policies for the first time, the 'checklist aspect' of the Charter should be particularly helpful. The report also acknowledges that well-managed tourism can significantly contribute to the development of the forthcoming National Park Plan, and to the aims as laid outing the National Parks (Scotland) Act 2000.

Basis for Strengthening Relationships

Charter Principles 3 'To involve all those directly implicated by tourism, its development and management, in and around the protected area,' provides the justification for bringing together tourism organisations; private sector interests; NPA's; development agencies; and community and conservation interests; in a permanent forum (or equivalent arrangement). That is particularly relevant, due to the completely of the administrative boundaries in both parks. It will also provide an on-going mechanism for these stockholder interest to be involved in how the park is developed, managed and promoted for tourism.

Raising the Profile of the Parks and Sustainable Tourism

The charter will raise the profile of the Parks within tourism planning for the area, and of tourism within the overall planning and management of the Park.

Publicity attached to the award of the Charter can be beneficial locally and the Charter can be used to promote the Park, particularly to European markets, where environmental issues are increasingly important.

Influencing Tourism Development

The strategy that is produced as part of the process will provide future guidance on tourism development.

Internal an external Assessment

The Charter process and verification procedures will provide an objective assessment of strengths, weaknesses, opportunities and threats facing the Parks.

Influence on Funding Bodies

Adherence to the Charter will support funding applications, and specific funding needs will be identified during the development of the strategy.

Networking with Other Parks

There are considerable opportunities for parks to share experiences with the other Charter Parks and the report provides case studies to illustrate specific issues.

Issues for the Scottish Parks to consider for Stockholders Engagement. The role of the NPA and level of commitment by partners. When the NPA is fully established, its role with regard to sustainable tourismness to be clearly agreed and defined. The Charter expects the NPA to have ultimate responsibility for the strategy although this could be effected through a partnership organisation of which the NPA was a member. It is important that a sufficient level of commitment to sustainable tourism is shows by the NPA and key partners and staff resources and budgets must be adequate to meet the requirements of developing and implementing a sustainable tourism strategy. This also means sufficient time to consult with stockholders, and the Europe are report provides feedback from the initial Charter parks on the time and resource input to achieve Charter status.

Although not a specific requirement, a core working group may be appropriated executive level to work on implementing the strategy through the action plan.

Involving Individual Tourism Stockholders

The report identifies a number of approaches that could be considered such as working through the ATB's and their membership; a Park-wide Association and links with sector groupings e.g. existing networks of tourism providers but acknowledges that further work on this is required. This is particularly important with regard to the number of tour operators and associated hotels that are present in each area. In due course this element will be the third section of the Charter, but founding or resources for developing it are not currently available.

Involving Wider Stockholders Interests

The verification for the Charter specifically points to the involvement of community and local conservation interests, and although there is considerable evidence of awareness by local community groups in both Parks, more though needs to be given to the parallel involvement of local conservation interests.

Relationships with National Bodies

It is a requirement of the Charter that it is used to raise the profile of the Parks at national level and the report recommends that the involvement of Visit Scotland and SNH should be continued.

Developing Networks of sustainable Tourism Businesses

this is about the second element of the Charter which has not been developed at European level, but involves encouraging tourism enterprises to abide by a set of sustainable tourism principles. Eurparc is encouraging parks to consider how they can utilise existing national environmental accreditation schemes, and the parks should encourage participation in such schemes (eg the Green Tourism Business Scheme) and possibly the development of networks of accredited enterprises overtime.

Developing Communication Processes

Communication with all stockholders is extremely important and mechanisms should be developed to keep tourism enterprises and other interests aware of the ongoing work and opportunities open to them.

A local undergraduate has offered to do some research as part of her final year thesis of a BA in Tourism and it is felt that additional investigation into the involvement of the wider stockholders interests and communication processes would be particularly valuable at this stage.

Development of Strategy

The sustainable tourism strategy and five-year action plan provides the main basis on which the Charter application is judged. Normally this would be a stand alone document but it could form part of a National Park Plan provided it was a substantial separate section. The strategy should address:

Protection and enhancement of environment and heritage

- Economic and social development
- Maintenance of quality of life
- Providing visitor satisfaction

The process of preparing the strategy is an important as its contents and should involve consultation with all stockholders.

The Europearc report identifies the key tourism strategies that exist in each area and how these might be drawn into a Park strategy.

There are a number of areas of action that the Charter

expects to be addressed by the parks within the strategy and these are contained in the following principles:

- Protecting and enhancing the natural and cultural heritage
- Understanding and meeting visitor needs and ensuring quality
- Communicating the Special Qualities of the Area
- Encouraging tourism products relating to the protected area
- Training relating to the protected area and sustainable tourism
- Maintaining the local quality of life
- Increasing benefit to the local economy

Monitoring and influencing visitor flows

The Europeare report expands each of the principles and gives brief examples of relevant current activity and projects in the two parks.

The Europarc report highlights the considerable interest that was shown during the consultation for the research and suggests that consideration of the Charter process as a possible way forward for sustainable tourism in both Park areas by key partners will now need to take place. For the Cairngorms there is specific reference to the need to sustain momentum during the interim period of the National Park Authority and the importance of continuing the involvement of the Area Tourist Boards.

Theme Park Tips

What do I need to know before I make may reservations at the Park?

- To avoid disappointment and/or a psychotic break, call ahead when planning your trip to see if any of the big rides will be closed due to scheduled maintenance during your stay. You don't want to get all the way there only to find out that Wally World is closed while you're in town.

- Make a plan before you go. Get a list of the rides and/or a map of the Park and include everyone in the planning. Some of the parks are so large; you may not be able to see everything even if you have more than one day at the Park. Some of the rides are so awesome: you may want to try to ride them more than once.
- Remember that some of the rides have height restrictions. Many rides also have health warnings for items such as pregnancy, bad backs or heart trouble. Motion sickness and scare factors also need to be considered when planning your Park rides. It is better to plan in advance than to build up a ride as a must see only to find a restriction that will keep some from going on the ride.
- Before you make all your other reservations, you might want to call ahead to find out about any special Park events such as parades, light shows, live music or TV and movie filming that are taking place around the time of your vacation. You might find something special enough to warrant changing the dates of your vacation.
- Many Parks have longer hours during certain days. Check to see if you can make it on one of those days.

Question Index

How can I get special treatment or discounts at the Park?

- Check with your company, other associations and memberships to see if they have any connections. Many of the Park rides or events have corporate sponsorship; you might to be entitled to a special seating, VIP lounge or be allowed to skip to the front of the line.

- Check to see if your trip could be planned during a second day free period.

Question Index

What is the best day to go?

- Check the Parks opening times, they do change. Some Parks will open earlier or close later on certain days thus giving you more bang for the buck.
- Disney World offers early entry to certain Parks on certain days to those staying in Disney Hotels. Find out which Parks open early on what days, and use this information to your advantage. If you're staying at Disney,
- Take advantage of this early entry. If you're not staying at Disney, avoid the early entry Parks, they will be filled with the Disney hotel guests.
- Sometimes the Parks will have light shows, fireworks, and parades or live music only on certain days. The Parks publish schedules with this information. These can be found by directly contacting the Parks and are also available at some tourist information centers and local hotels.

Question Index

What should I wear?

- Forget high fashion, you want to be able to enjoy all your days at the Parks.
- Wear cool and comfortable clothing. Light colors will help to reflect the sun's rays. Natural fibers breathe the most and will dry the quickest. Since many of the Parks have water rides that are designed to get you wet and cool you off; you might want

to also consider the see through factor of your clothing if it gets wet.

- Wear cool, comfortable and supportive shoes. You are going to spend a lot of time on your feet, either walking or standing in line. Bring an extra set of shoes to leave in your car in case one pair gets wet.
- Cover you body with a strong sunscreen. The Florida sun is very strong and you'll be exposed to it for much of the day. If you want to take a tan home, build it slowly. A burn will ruin your whole trip.
- Use some baby powder with cornstarch to help keep your feet and other body parts dry. Try this before you leave to make sure your skin isn't overly sensitive to the powder.
- Consider bringing a hat and sunglasses. They can also help keep you cool and save you from burning. But, you'll have to hold on to them the whole day, so don't bring the ones you'll be upset about losing. You could also look into buying those little ropes to hold your glasses on while you ride.
- Avoid wearing jewelry or other loose items that could get caught or become uncomfortable on the rides.

Question Index

What extra items do I need to bring with me?

- You might want to bring along a freezer bag to seal in your wallet for those water rides.
- Consider bringing raingear. Central Florida, the Theme Park capital of the world, is famous for quick, heavy showers. During the afternoon heat of the day, usually from June to September you can have clear skies one minute and a total downpour

the next. These are usually short term, so you might get lucky and just duck inside for a while. Check the local forecast to see if you'll need it for a few minutes or hours.

- Bring an extra pair of comfortable shoes and socks.
- You might bring a collapsible plastic water cup to assist you at the drinking fountains.
- Consider bring a fanny pack to do the work of carrying all the items you'll need.
- If you have two adults in your group, you might consider bringing an extra set of car keys.
- When and where should I get my tickets?
- Get your tickets ahead of time to avoid the line at the gate.
- Only purchase your tickets from the Parks themselves or their authorized agents.
- Approach any special deals with caution. There are ticket scams out there.

Question Index

What are some of the ticket scams I should know about?

- PSSSST, buddy, is not a good way to spend you vacation dollars.
- There are counterfeit, copy and lots of other scams out there.
- Some of the Parks have second day free tickets, which get resold to unsuspecting tourists who get turned away at the gate since they are not the same people who purchased the original tickets. The

Parks do check your I.D.

- Beware the handling fees. Some places will offer discounts only to require a large handling fee that will take back you discount. Ask for the total ticket price including all taxes and fees. You might be better off buying them directly from the Park. Also, many ticket distributors charge a hefty restocking fee if you return the tickets. Avoid these places unless you are positive you wont' be returning them.
- Although they aren't a scam, many discount tickets are sold with the requirement that you attend a sales presentation. You can save money with these tickets, but make sure you are aware of the commitment necessary to get the discount. You'll want to consider if the discount is worth your time and if you have any interest in the product they are selling.
- Check for restrictions, some tickets are only valid on certain days or during certain time periods.
- As always, if it sounds too good to be true it probably is. Approach any special deals with caution.
- How can I get the most out of my time at the Park?
- Go off-season when the Parks are less crowded, but check the Park's hours to make sure they haven't cut too much time out of your day.
- Go on days when the Park is open extra hours.
- Check the daily attendance records and go on the lighter days.
- Surprisingly, the weekend may be less crowded

since many are using the weekend as traveling days for their weeklong vacations.

- Plan ahead and come prepared.
- Get there early
- Use the tip board for a specific information.
- Use the map when you plan to avoid crisscrossing.
- Take a restroom break whenever you are close to a restroom. Don't follow the crowd, look for the road less traveled. Many people will go to the right and move clock wise throughout the Park. Check into going left and moving counterclockwise.
- Eat during the off-hours.
- Be kind to your body

Question Index

When should I get there?

- Arrive early, at least a ½ hour before they open. Some parks will allow you to enter even earlier. You will not be able to get on the rides early, but you might be first in line.
- You'll get a good Parking place and many of the Parks will let you into the Park a little earlier then the published opening times.
- This is also a good way to get a great spot inline for the most popular rides.
- Eat a good breakfast before you go. You'll need the energy, but be sure to leave time for the meal to settle before you get to the Park.

Question Index

Will Parking be a problem?

- This will depend on which Park you attend.
- Many Parks chare for parking, so make sure to include this in your budget.
- Most Parks have enough parking, so you biggest problem probably won't be finding a space, but finding your way back to it at the end of the day.
- Most Parks use characters and/or colors to label their parking lot sections. Remember where you park, even if you have to write your section's name down. There are over 11,000 parking spaces at Disney's Magic Kingdom alone.
- Theme Park's parking lots tend to be filled with lots o similar looking rental cars hiding behind the largest collection of minivans you've ever seen. Again, write your section's name down.

Question Index

What should I do as soon as I get to the Park?

- Ask the ticket taker for the location o the tip board and get a Park map.
- Rent a stroller or wheelchair if you need them. These services are generally available at the very front of the park.
- Plan on mixing outdoor rides within door or cooler water rides in each section of the Park. Mix in rides that give you lots of sitting time, between the rides where you'll be standing inline for long periods of time. This will provide you with breaks and help you to stay cool.
- Check out the tip board for parade routes, character appearances, time and other helpful information on rides such as wait times, hours open, eight, age and health restrictions.
- Be sure to note the location of lost and found, restaurants, water foundations and restrooms on

the Park's map.

- You should look through the map's index of the Park's restaurants and see if you can decide on a place to eat. You might want to check them out first so you'll know to look for them when you are in a particular area of the Park. If there is a particular place you want to eat, you don't want to waste all you time waling across the Park to get there. Make a plan that will leave you in that area when it is time to eat.
- You should also locate the Parks restrooms while you have the map out so that you'll be abie to take advantage of them when one is in the area. Agree on a meeting place if you get separated.

Question Index

How do e know where to go if we get separated?

- While you're still all together and you have the map out, find a central meeting place for everyone in case you get separated.
- Remember that some of the good central landmarks like Cinderella's Castle are quite large, so be specific. Make the meeting place in front of the Castle, next to the pond closest to Tomorrow land and make sure everyone knows how to get there.

Question Index

How can I get the best spot to see the parade?

If you love a parade, state out your spot early since they usually draw crowds.

Check the tip board or Park map to find the parade route.

- Picking an incline might allow you a better view of the whole parade.
- This way you can look down on the whole parade

as it comes toward you.

- Picking a spot toward the beginning of the parade will provide you a jump on everyone else. You will have finished watching the parade and made it to the most popular rides while most of the crowd is still watching the parade.
- Make sure to check out your spot with a Park employee, you don't want to wait half an hour, only to be moved to the back of the crowd because you perfect spot is in the middle of the parade route.
- Pick the side of the street you want to be on when the parade ends. The parade route may block you access to areas you want to be in until after the parade is over.
- When is the best time to eat?
- Eat a good breakfast before you get to the Park. One there, try to eat earlier or after than most. Eat while the restaurants are empty around everyone else is crowded on the rides. If you don't care for a parade, skip it and eat. Everyone else will crowd the parade route and leave the restaurants empty. If you eat during the off hours, you won't waste your time in line at the restaurant and you'll be able to ride with shorter lines while all the others are eating.

Question Index

How can I make a day at the Them Park easier on my body?

- Drink plenty of water throughout the day. You might not want to pay soft drink prices for the bottled water, but plenty of water will help your body to make it through the day.
- You can get really hot, but avoid the temptation to

gulp down really cold water. This quick shock to your body can be very dangerous.

- Pay attention to ride height and healthy restrictions; they are there for a reason. If you try to sneak in when you were advised not to ride and ignore the posted warnings, you may end up suffering for the rest of your trip.
- You should consider mixing some indoor shows, or theater rides with outdoors or action rides. This will give you some much needed little breaks to sit down and cool off throughout the day.
- If you don't think you can make it for a whole day at the park, you might consider breaking up your time there with a mid-afternoon break instead of just leaving early. This break could allow you to spend more time in the Park throughout your day. The night usually brings lower temperatures and thinking crowds, so it will be easier on you to enjoy the Park. Don't forget to get you hand stamped, also keep your ticket and your Parking pass.
- You'll be tempted with lots of tasty treats all day. Remember that you body is already stressed by all the activity so try to fit some healthy food into you day. Rich foods are more difficult for your body to digest.
- If a particular food sometimes upsets you stomach, stay away from it at the Park. The rides are designed to toss you around, but they don't want you to toss back.
- Don't save the water rides for last or you'll have a soggy ride home.

Question Index

How can I keep all the souvenirs I buy from weighting me down?

- When buying souvenirs, remember you might have to carry them around all day. Check with the Park to see if there are any other options available before you get to loaded down.
- You might hold off your purchases until the end of the day. Many Park's will close their rides, but still leave their sops open for a while. This will also allow the Parking lot some time to thin out.
- Some of the parks will hold your purchase to pick up at the front gate when you leave.
- Some Parks can arrange for delivery to your local hotel or your home address.
- Many Parks have lockers available. If you've rented a stroller, use it to help with some of the heavy carrying, but don't leave packages on you stroller when you leave the stroller unsupervised.

Question Index

What should I do if I get too tired and decide I need to leave?

If you think you've had enough and it's time to leave, get you hand stamped. A little rest, a show ever and you might feel like returning, especially since it cools off a little after sunset and the crowds thin out. Most of the Parks have a grand finale show such as a big parade, light show, and fireworks or live action thriller. These are often spectacular and if you can't make the whole day, you might consider coming back so you don't miss one of the best parts of the Park. You'll want to keep you ticket and Parking pass since most Parking passes are good for the whole day.

CHAPTER SEVEN

Nature based Tourism and Parks

Nature-based tourism is travel dependent upon the attributes of the natural environment. This chapter discusses the nature-based tourism market globally, and more specifically the segment of this tourism occurring in parks and protected areas. Nature-based tourism is the travel and tourism activity dependent upon the destination attributes of the natural environment.

This tourism is dependent upon two fundamental components:

(a) appropriate levels of environment quality and

(b) suitable levels of consumer service.

Nature-based tourism has become sufficiently large that sub-markets are becoming apparent. Eagles (1995a) suggests, using a motive-based methodology for segmentation, that the nature-tourism market contains at least fur recognizable niche markets; eco-tourism, wilderness use, adventure travel and car camping. Ecotourism involves travel for the discovery of and learning about wild, natural environments Wilderness travel involves personal re-creation through primitive travel in natural environments that are devoid of human disturbance. Adventure travel is personal accomplishment through the trills of dominating dangerous environments. Car camping is safe, family travel in the interface between the wild and the civilized (Eagles, 1995a). This classification utilizes unique sets of social motives to identify the market segments. Each of the niche markets at a different stage in the typical business cycle (Figure1.2) us in Butler's (1980) tourism life cycle analysis approach. Ecotourism and adventure tourism have considerable growth potential, according to this analysis. Wilderness travel is reaching capacity in many locales because of th erequirement of very low-density level use in wilderness destinations. Car camping is probably in deeline, or soon will be, largely due to the peak population profile of the developed world passing beyond the ages in which camping is popular. All four of these market segments are visible in part tourism internationally. Given the different travel motivation sets in each submarkets, it is important for planners and managers to be aware of the implications for park visitor management.

For example, the levels of social grouping, the level of desired service, the level of environmental quality and the desired environmental attributes vary amongst the four sub-markets. For detail refer in Eagles (1995a), but it is important to note that such differences only become visible with the large and growing size of the nature-based tourism market. Nature-based tourism is a large and growing component of international tourism. Several countries in the world have nature-based tourism as a key component of their most important export industry, tourism. These countries include Australia, Kenya, Nepal, New Zealand, Tanzania, Costa Rica, and Botswana; to name a few. Anyone country has global competition in this field and this competition is becoming more sophisticated each year. The economic importance of the tourism industries in these countries is leading to more thoughtful policy and institutional development. It is important to recognize the constructive role that can be played by positive and consultative policy development in nature-based and park tourism. Three important examples are Australia, Tanzania and New Zealand.

The national ecotourism strategy for Australia succinctly summarizes the background to the aggressive and successful policy development in that country:

> Ecotourism offers the potential to generate foreign exchange earnings, employment, and other economic and social benefits, particularly in regional areas. It presents Australia with the opportunity to make the most of its competitive advantage, with its spectacular and diverse natural features, unique flora and fauna and diverse cultural heritage. Ecotourism can also provide resources for environmental conservation and management and an incentive for the conservation and sustainable use of public and private land (Allcc et al., 1994, a. 5).

To ensure the success of the national policy, the Australian government committed Aus. $10,000,000 over four years for the implementation of the strategy. Following the national lead, each state started to develop a similar regional policy, the latest being the one for New South Wales (Worboys, 1997).

Tanzania has a draft national tourism policy document, an integrated aster plan, and an infrastructure plan. A key part of this plan is to develop a southern tourism loop to exploit the national parks and wildlife reserves, such as Ruaha national park and selous Game Reserve, in the southern part of the country. This new loop will complement the very successful northern loop that contains sites such as Kilimanjaro National Park, the Serengetti National park, and the Ngorongoo Conservation Area (wade, 1998). New Zealand has a very successful nature-based tourism policy that involves high levels of public and private cooperation in the protection of landscapes, the management of protected areas, and the delivery of tourism services. These countries have government policy as the framework for a whole range of public and private activities, and this policy has helped foster a suitable environment for the development of nature-based tourism generally, and park tourism specifically. Government policy plays a very important role in the development of tourism industries that are financially and ecologically sustainable.

The goal of this chapter is to descrietrends in international in park tourism globally. Implications for tourism planners and managers are discussed.

The existing literature on park tourism provides background. Access to unpublished documents and data sources of the Protected Area Data Unit of the World Conservation Monitoring Centre in Cambridge, UK allowed for the inclusion of up-to-date information on the status of the world's parks and protected areas. Secondary data analysis of a national survey of Canadian park finance (Van Sicle and Eagles, 1998) provided information on finance, budget and operational policies within that country. Access to a North American data base under development on visitor use in parks allowed for presentation of current tourism levels (Eagles, McLean and Stabler, 2000). These North American examples are used because of the depth of the information available, and because they illustrate important principles that have a wider utility. Conservations with scholars and managers of park tourism, from many countries, contributed contextual and trend information. The preparation of this chapter involved site visits to observe park tourism in the following countries: Australia, Canada, Costa Rica, Cuba, Ecuador, Kenya, Lesotho, New Zealand, Mexico, Slovenia, Switzerland, South Africa, Tanzaniam, The United Kingdom of Great Britain, the Untied States of America, and Venezuela.

Trends in Park Establishment

Globally, the area of land covered by the world's parks and protected areas increased considerable from 1900 to 1996. B 1996 the world's network of 30,361 parks covers an area of 12, 245,527 square kilometers, representing 8.84% of the totally and area of the planet. This total land area occurs in 225 countries and dependent territories (Green & Paine, 1997). Figure 2.3 shows the growth of this network over a 100-year period. The impressive growth of the world's park network is the result of the widespread acceptance of the ecological ethic (Kellert, 1979) and aggressive political action. It appears that the tourism activity occurring at these sites created a self-perpetuating phenomenon of visitation, education, and desire for more parks, visitation and education.

The global network includes a wide variety of types of protected areas, ranging from nature reserve through to protected landscape, within the International Union for the Conservation of Nature and Natural Resources' (IUCN) six-category system (IUCN, 1994).Within this system, the categories vary according to the level of human development allowed, with Category I having least human impact and Category VI. The management categories' system provides a common international standard for classifying the many different types of protected area designation in countries around the world, based on the primary management objective. This facilitates accounting and monitoring to national, regional and international levels. Global network listed by management category. All six categories are well represented in the network, but with national parks and resource management areas being the two categories with highest representation in the system. National Parks, Category II, is a prominent and well-known land classification covering 2.67% of the earth's land surface. A very significant amount of the world's most significant biodiversity conservation sites is located in Category I and II sites. However, all sites play some role.

IUCN Categories and Definitions for Protected Areas

Category 1	Strict nature reserve/ Wilderness Area: protected area managed mainly for science or wilderness protection.
Category 1a	Strict Nature Reserve: protected area managed mainly for science.
Definition:	Area of land and/or sea possessing some outstanding or representative ecosystems, geological or physiological features and/or species, available primarily for scientific research and/or environmental monitoring.
Category II	National Park: protected area managed mainly for ecosystem protection and recreation.
Definition:	Natural area of land and/or sea, designated to (a) protect the ecological integrity of one or more ecosystems for present and future generations, (b) exclude exploitation or occupation inimical to the purposes of designation of the area, and (c) provide a foundation for spiritual, scientific, educational, recreational and visitor opportunities, all of which must be environmentally and cultural compatible.
Category III	Natural Monument: protected area managed mainly for conservation of specific natural features.
Definition:	Area containing one, or more, specific natural or natural/cultural features which is of outstanding or unique value because of its inherent rarity, representative or aesthetic qualities or cultural significance.
Category IV	Habitat/species Management Area: protected area managed mainly for conservation through management intervention.
Definition:	Area of land and/or sea subject to active intervention for management purposes so as to ensure the maintenance of habitats and/or to meet the requirements of specific species.

Category V	Protected Landscape/Seascape: protected area managed mainly for landscape/seascape conservation and recreation.
Definition:	Area of land, with coast and sea as appropriate, where the interaction of people and nature over time had produced an area of distinct character with significant aesthetic, ecological and/or cultural value, and often with high biological diversity. Safeguarding the integrity of this traditional interaction is vital to the protection, maintenance and evolution of such an area.
Category VI	Managed Resource Protected Area; protected area managed mainly for the sustainable use of natural ecosystems.
Definition:	Area containing predominantly unmodified natural systems, managed to ensure long-term protection and maintenance of biological diversity, while providing at the same time a sustainable flow of natural products and services to meet community needs.

Note: Adapted from Green and Payne (1997) and IUCN (1994).

The name national park is closely associated with nature-based tourism, being a system of a high quality natural environment with a well-designed tourist infrastructure. Eagles and Wind (1994) found that Canadian ecotour companies frequently used the name national park as a brand name to attract potential ecotourists to their sales offerings. With 30,361 parks in the word, and with 3,386 having the well-known name of a national park, it is clear that any particular political unit, such as one country or one province within a country, has a major task to get its sites precognized globally. There is a very large number of sites available for tourists. Some countries, such as Canada, have the disadvantage of having many of their sites known as provincial parks, a name unknown outside Canada, and suggestive of a lower level of importance.

Unfortunately, there is no global tabulation of park usage, as there is for park area. Therefore, it is not possible to comprehensively report on the total volume of recreational use in recent years or its change over time. However, individual country reports and the personal communication wit many scholars and park managers suggest that park tourism volume has increased considerably over time (Filion, Foley, & Jaquemot, 1994; Driml, & Common, 1995; Wells, 1997; Eagles, & Higgins, 1998). Recent trends from Costa Rica National Parks; a typical curve showing increases over time. The decline was due to a weak economy in the US causing lowered travel to Costa Rica combined with an 800% increase in park entrance fees for foreigners.

Table 7.1: Global Protected Areas classified by IUCN Management Category

	Protected Areas Globally					
IUCN Category	*Number*	*Percent*	*Total Area im km²*	*Percent*	*Mean area in km2*	*Percent total land area of the world*
Ia. Nature Reserve	4,395	14	982,487	7	224	0.66
Ib. Wilderness	806	3	940,344	7	1,167	0.63
II. National Park	3,386	11	4,000,825	30	1,182	2.67
III. Natural Monument	2,122	7	193,022	1	91	0.13
IV. Habitat Area	11,171	37	2,460,283	19	220	1.64
V. Protected Landscape	5,584	18	1,067,118	8	191	0.71
VI. Resource Management	2,897	10	3,601,447	27	1,243	2.4
Total	30,361	100	13,245,528	99	436	8.84.

Eagles, McLean and Sabler (2000) calculated the total

national and provincial/state park usage in North America. In 1996 there was an estimated 2,621,777,237 visitor days of recreation activity in the parks and protected areas of Canada and the US. Clearly, the outdoor recreation occurring in the parks and protected areas in Canada and the United States is a very large and impressive activity. With an estimated 2.6 billion days of use per year this activity has major economic, social and environmental impacts.

However, until there are international standards for park tourism data collection and management, and global tabulation of these data, this important international activity will suffer from a lack of co-ordination in data reporting and an associated void in public policy profile.

Park Economics

Economics is an important component of societal decision-making, but it is often given low priority in the parks' world (Wells, 1997; Van Sickle & Eagles, 1998). Usually in parks, the very strong emphasis given to ecology is seen by many park proponents as sufficient justification for public policy action. However, nature tourism is increasingly becoming important within sustainable development because of the potential of contributing to local and national economic development while also providing incentive for nature conservation and biodiversity conservation (Wells, 1997; Lindberg, 1998).

Most of the world's protected areas charge low entry and use fees. These fees typically cover only a portion of the cost of protecting the resource and providing the features on which developed during a period where resource protection was seen as the overwhelmingly important objective, a public objective that benefits all of society. If a public good benefits all, it can be reasonably argued that it should be paid for by taxes on society. However, this logic falters when applied to outdoor recreation in parks as only those who participate in outdoor recreation area beneficiaries. In a time of widespread government financial retrenchment, it is increasingly difficult to justify public expenditure to subsidize the recreation of one segment of the population. Governments around the world are using this logic, in part, for the reduction or freezing of grants for park management. The reduction of budgets has been documented in Canada and the USA (Eagles, 1995b) as has the development of new forms of park administration and new pricing policies (Van Sickle and Eagles, 1998). The Parks Canada business plan summarizes this concept with the statement that "subsidies will be phased out on services of benefit to individuals, by transferring the operation to the nonprofit voluntary or private sectors, or these services will be stabilized on a full cost recovery basis" (Parks Canada, 1995, p. 7).

There are dramatic differences amongst the world's parks in terms of pricing policy, tourism income, and financial management. A global study of biosphere reserves found that only 32 of 78 responding sites charged visitors admission fees (Tye and Gordon, 1995). The fees ranged from less than $5.00 to $110 per person per day, in US funds, with the vast majority at the lower range. There was a statistically significant relationship between total direct income and the numbers of visitors for all biosphere reserves. Higher visitor numbers corresponded to higher budgets. The authors concluded that "better financed biosphere reserves are likely to be better managed, thereby attracting more tourists" (Tye and Gordon, 1995, p. 29). Presumably those reserves with more tourists gained higher political profile. This political strength allowed the sites to argue for more budget allocation from government. Some sites also earned income from user fees. This study is important because it shows a strong and positive relationship between protected areas' budgets and tourism levels. Generally, those parks with high levels of tourism clients gain higher levels of political power. This power is then translated into higher budget allocations. It is important to recognize that substantial management budgets are necessary in areas of high usage to avoid excessive damage to the natural environment of the parks.

Parks often supply the most important part of the nature tourism experience, but typically capture little of the economic value of the stream of economic benefits (Wells, 1997). The low entry and use fees in parks are the result of many factors, one being the effort of a centralized budget allocation process in many governments. With this form of government financial management, the park management does not keep earned fees within its internal financial structure, and therefore sees little benefit in comprehensive fee collection. This also contributes to a low emphasis on park visitor management. Such issues as return rates, length of stay, visit satisfaction and service quality all suffer when the financial return from the visitors is not tied directly to the financial operation of a park. This lack of proper emphasis on visitor management results in a dwarfed park tourism industry, one not fulfilling its potential.

Many governments see nature-based tourism as an important tool for economic development. Unfortunately, most have not invested sufficiently in a staff training, infrastructure or park resources that are needed to support nature tourism. This exposes sensitive sites to tourism-caused degradation (Wells, 1997).

Most national tourism agencies do not keep statistics on market sectors, such as those associated with nature-based tourism and park-based tourism. Other management units, such as park agencies seldom fill this information void. As a result, important sectors, such as nature-based tourism, are not clearly documented for the benefit of policy determination. Looking at the Canadian situation can show this situation. Clearly nature-based tourism is one of the key elements of Canadian tourism. Filion et al. (1994) estimated that as much as one quarter of the tourism expenditures in Canada can be attributed to wildlife tourism, one of the elements of nature tourism. The Canadian Tourism Commission provides quarterly Canadian tourism figure to governments, business and the media. These data considerably raise the profile of tourism within the business sector. However, in Canada there is not system for the collection and distribution of information on nature-based or park-based tourism. Neither the volumes of park visitation nor its economic impacts are systematically collected and made available for government and private consumption. Therefore, the importance of nature tourism in the country is severely underrated due to lack of adequate information. The parks do not compare well to other economic generators, such as auto manufacturing or forestry, where the volumes and economic value of the products are carefully documented and reported within a continuous stream of information. This Canadian situation is common throughout the world. The economic impact of park tourism is not well known, not well documented, and where known, not well communicated. This leads to a severe under-representation of the importance of park tourism within the fiscal sectors of government and business.

Wells (1997) documented, globally, the economic studies available on nature tourism. Most of these studies are of individual parks or wildlife reserves. There are few regional or national studies of the economic impact of the tourism associated with parks and reserves.

Eagles, McLean & Stabler (2000) compiled a national park-used database for Canada and the United States. They found that in 1996, the last year complete data were available, 2,506,451,728 visitor days of recreation occurred in the federal and state parks and protected areas of the USA, and an additional 115,325,509 visitor days of recreation occurred in Canadian federal and provincial protected areas. This massive volume of 2,621,777,237 visitor days, previously undocumented, reveals in high level of tourism use not generally known and appreciated. The economic implications of the usage are normally not calculated and therefore are certainly not well known in the fiscal policy areana of North American society. It is useful to look at some of the park tourism economic impact studies that have been done, against using Canada and the USA as case studies.

Ontario has a large and well-used provincial park system consisting of 275 parks. In 1992 the total economic output from park users and by government was Can. $831,200,000 (OMNR and Econometric Research, 1993). A total of 12,172 person-yeas of employment resulted from parks. This benefit was calculated from data on the 109 parks that were staffed to manage visitor use in 1992. More economic benefit would be found if the other non-staffed, 166 provincial parks, the six national parks and the hundreds of conservation areas were added to the calculations.

Recent research documented the expenditure level of park users to Ontario's Algonquin Provincial Park (Bowman, 2001). This is Ontario's oldest and most visited Provincial Park. Table 1.3 shows that the expenditures per person per day varied dramatically, with day visitors spending the most, at $208.00 and car campers the least, at $27.7. This research showed that the park management earned the most income from the groups that spent the least per day, car and interior campers. Conversely, the management earned the least from the people who spent the most, day visitors and lodge visitors. Two important user groups, bus tour visitors and children's camp users were not studied. This analysis shows the need for a complete re-evaluation of the pricing and income policy of this important park.

The provincial economic impact was calculated by the Provincial Economic Impact Model of the department of Canadian Heritage. The impact generated by Algonquin

Park and friends of Algonqun organizational spending was estimated as Can $4.9 million in labour income, $6.0 million to the Gross Domestic Product and 150 full-time person-years of employment. The provincial economic impact generated by visitor spending was estimated as $8,1 million in labour income, $11.9 million to the Gross Domestic Product and 301 full-time person-years of employment. Therefore, the provincial economic impact generated by park expenditures, Friends expenditures and expenditures by five visitor groups (day users, can campers, interior campers, lodge visitors, and cottage leaseholders) was $13 million in labour, $17.9 in GDP and 451in person years of employment. This is a conservative estimate.

Parks Ontario typically uses the Ministry of Natural Resources Social and Economic Impact model for estimates of economic impact of the provincial parks (D. Mulrooney, personal communication, September 17, 1997). Information from this model is used for budget planning, local political promotión and sales of park products. However, this effort is modest in scope and not widely applied.

The most recent economic benefits study for a park system undertaken in Canada was done for British Columbia (Coopers & Lybrand, 1995). The study concluded that the BC provincial parks' system is a major source of economic activity in the province. In 1993 the parks generated 5,300 jobs directly and 4,000 jobs indirectly. The 5,300 jobs created by parks are comparable to other industries such as newsprint (4,2000),, metal mining (3,800) and coal mining (3,000). In 1993 the BC provincial parks' system contributed about Can. $430,000,000 to the provincial gross domestic product. The park visitors reported significant benefits from recreational activities beyond the market transactions. These nonmarket benefits were estimated at Can. $670,000,000 beyond the cost of operating the system by the province. Clearly, British Columbia's provincial parks are a major economic force in the province. If the national parks' contribution was added to the BC provincial park's contribution, then the benefits would be considerably enhanced.

The Province of Alberta under too an economic impact calculation of tourism in its provincial parks, following on the lead of British Columbia. The results showed an economic impact that was large and similar to the economic impact of forestry in the province. The report was never officially released. It is speculated that the significance of the information to decision making resulted in a successful lobby effort by the forest industry to make sure that the report was not released, in order to avoid the positive political impact that would occur to parks with the report's dissemination. This is a common problem for park managers, interagency conflict that results in a suppression of data and resources with the goal of now allowing park tourism to gain the full public policy profile that it would otherwise enjoy. This is especially an issue when park management is within a broadly-defined resource management agency. This is least of an issue when parks are a stand alone agency or administration.

Parks Canada conservatively estimates the economic impact of national pars, national historic sites and parks, and national canals to Canada's GDP at Can. $1,250,000 per year. Around 30,000 person-years of employment occur due to this spending. Non-resident visitors contribute 255 of the visitor spending, or S275,000,000 annually (Parks Canada, 1995). Coopers & Lybrand Consulting (1995) calculated that in 1993 British Columbia provincial parks produced total benefits of Can. $430,000,000. These benefits included direct benefits, and consumer surplus. In 1993 the parks had 22,300,000 visitor days of activity. Therefore, each day of recreation produced an economic benefit of Can. $19. in 1992 the total economic output due to Ontario parks was Can. $831,200,000 (OMNR and Econometric Research, 1993). This amount included direct, indirect, and induced impacts of parks. In 1992 Ontario provincial parks had 7,000,000 visitor days of recreation activity. Therefore, each day of recreation produced an economic benefit of Can. $119. The difference in calculated impact per person between B.C. and Ontario comes from different approaches to the calculation of impact. However, if one takes this range of economic benefits and papplies it to the visitation of all Canada's parks, an economic benefit occurs of between Can. $2.2 an #14 billion. However, which every figure is used, the implications of such a large economic impact on public policy making in Canada are immense. Clearly, a standard and consistent method of calculating economic impact is required, and one has been developed for the application by all provincial and national park agencies in Canada (Stanley, Person and Smeltzer, 1999).

If one assumes tat the 1996 figure of 2,621,777,237 entrnces to Cnadian and americna parks,as calculated by Eagles, Mcleanand Stabler (2000), represent visitor days of activity and one accepts an impact range of US $90 (OMNR and Econometric Research, 1993) to US $141 per day (Carlsen, 1997), the value for park tourism ranges between US $236 billion and $370 billion in Canada and the USA combined. These figures must be accepted with caution, given the limitations of the data. However, the estimation sdo show that park-based tourism is a very important economic activity in North American society. Even these high estimates underestimate value, because they do not include option, bequest or existence value estimates.

Impressive as these figures are, they have not convinced American and Canadian governments to maintain the tax-based grant levels upon which most of the park systems depend. Figure 5 shows the impacts of massive budget cuts on the 13 national, territorial, and provincial park systems in Canada over recent years (Van Sicle and eagles, 1998). All systems lost staff numbers. Ten closed facilities. Nine operated a smaller programme, did less maintenance on facilities, privatized services and undertook programme efficiencies, such as replacement of staff with mechanized processes. The management effectiveness of the park agencies in Canada was impaired by the budget cuts and by the associated reduction sin services and programmes.

Driml and Common (1995) showed that the economic benefits of nature-based tourism in selected Australian locales far exceed the government expenditures to manage the site. This research estimated the financial value of tourism in five Australian World Heritage Areas (Great Barrier Reef, Wet Tropics, Uluru National Park, Kakadu National Park, and Tasmanian Wilderness). The five areas studied experienced tourism expenditures in 1991/92 of Aus. $1,372,000,000. The total management budgets were Aus. $48,700,000, and the user fee income to the management agencies was Aus. $4,160,000. Therefore, the management budgets were only 3.5% of the tourist expenditure that occurred in the World Heritage Reas. The revenue raised by government through user fees represented only 8.5% of the government expenditures. This study shows the very high financial value of tourism in the five World Heritage Areas. It also reveals the low level of government expenditure for management, and the very low level of government cot recovery. Driml and Common (1995) question the ability of the existing management structure to maintain environmental quality in the face of large increases in tourism use. They point out that tourism research expenditures in Australia are very low compared to other economic generators such as agriculture and mining, both of which have a smaller national economic impact than tourism.

In Canada there are several financial structures within the federal and provincial park agencies. Some are government agencies. Others function like crown corporations. Figure 6 shows the range in cost recovery for the 13 senior government park agencies in Canada. The recovery of management costs from tourist charges varies from only 1% in British Colubia, to slightly more than 50% in Saskatchewan This variation is largely due to government policy dictating the financial structure of the agencies, not to the volume of tourism nor to the amount of area being managed (Van Sickle and Eagles, 1998). Those with the lowest level of cost recover had very weak tourism expertise within the park agencies, with the result that most tourism income was earned by the private sector. Those with the highest level of cost recovery had revenue retention within the agency, and some form of corporate operations. Goodwin et al. (1995a) found in three parks in India, Indonesia and Zimbabwe that the income from tourism was between 7% to 24% of total expenditures. Clearly, most parks in this sample have the majority of their budget coming from sources other than tourism income. However, globally the trend is for government to demand that parks earn much higher amounts of their budget from tourism sources. Corresponding to this is the development of forms of management, such as parastatals, that allow for park agencies to function with the efficiencies of a private corporation.

Parks Canada has designed a management structure that encourages increasing higher levels of cost recovery from tourists. To provide the management structure necessary to implement the new business approach, Parks Canada (1995) obtained government permission (a) to retain and reinvest all revenues, (b) to plan and operate on a multi-year, non-lapsing basis, (c) to increase non-tax revenues from products and services, (d) to borrow against future revenue, (e) to link revenues to costs, and (f) to depreciate assets. The new approach moves this government agency into a management style very similar to that of a corporation, a government-owned corporation or a parastatal. To implement this plan, new national parks' legislation was passed by the Canadian Parliament in 1998.

By fiscal year 2000/2001 Parks Canada had gross revenues of Can $84.7 million, a 111% increase since 1994/1995. Three sources of income were prominent revenue sources:

entry fees with $30.1 million, rentals and concessions with $14.3 million and camping fees with $10.9 million. These figures reveals that increase emphasis on revenue generation, associated structure resulted in significant revenue gains.

The Australian, American, Canadian, Ontario, and British Columbia studies show the significance of parks to economic life in those areas. However, generally there is a lack of national and provincial economic data on parks. This is a major imhabitor in public policy making across the world and in Canada. For park economics to have the policy impact that it warrants, there must be a continuous stream of up-to-date data provided. At the very least, yearly studies are required. However, quarterly figures provided to government, business and the media would be more useful and beneficial.

Park Finance and Pricing Policy

Typically, in most countries park pricing policy involves a flat fee for entrance, typically for a vehicle, or for facility use, such as for one campsite. In many cases no fess are charged, especially in low-use care as, in popular sites in the low seasons or in remote areas. The fees are modest and not subject to market forces. Recreation allocation is typically done by the first-come first-serve approach. In some parks fees are also charged by the park agency for specialized recreation services, equipment rental, accommodation, food services and souvenir sales.

Typically the income from tourism is well below the park budget, constituting a small percentage of the money used for management. Van Sickle and Eagles (1998) found in Canadian national and provincial park agencies that fees provided an overall average of 17% of the budgets, a very similar amount to the 18% found by Brademans and read nor (1987) for the USA. Saskatchewan is the national leader in Canada, earning 52% of expenditures in 1994-

1995. In contrast the British Columbia provincial parks' agency, with a very different administrative structure, recovered only 1% of revenues. Recent figures from state parks in the USA show that for 1998 33.8% of state park budgets were recovered from various types of tourism fees (McLean, 1999). These figures from the USA suggest that in this country state parks are successfully earning higher percentages of their budgets from tourism fees. Globally, there is a trend of governments requiring parks to recover higher percentages of their budgets from tourist expenditures.

Often the generation of small amounts of revenue provides little incentive for the central government to provide adequate levels of budget for management. Laarman and Gregersen (1994) point out that this situation leads to a vicious cycle of "low fees, inadequate revenue, and deficient public investment – followed by continued low fees, revenue and investment." The typical budget situation for parks is that of a central government body setting an annual budget, dependent upon the money available for the central treasury as well as various political and lobby group machinations. Goodwin et al. (1995a) found in studies of parks in India, Indonesia and Zimbabwe there was no direct relationship between park budgets and park tourism revenues. In these three countries the money was collected locally, then submitted to central government.

In countries without a large tax-based subsidy for park management, tourism is often the largest source of income for park agencies. Throughout Africa, for example, the parks must earn much or most of their operating budgets from tourism. This has led to a level of innovation in pricing policy that is worthy of note.

South Africa has a booming tourism industry that has expanded dramatically n the past five years and is predicted to grow substantially in the next five years. Significantly, 60% of the 5.5 million tourists who visited the country in 1997 visited a national park or game reserve (Eagles, 1999). The democratically elected government of South Africa has man social objectives calling for budget allocation. As a result all tax-based grants to the national and provincial park systems are being phased out, leaving the parks with the options of increasing income from tourism or cutting staff and services. The parks are responding with impressive pricing and tourism service innovation.

The South African National parks (SANP) system is now at 80% budget recovery from tourism (Msimang, personal communication, May 21, 1999). SANP now operates an impressive array of tourism businesses in the national parks. It provides a range of accommodation, ranging from campgrounds through family cabins to hotels. All of the food and souvenir stores are agency operated. Many of the tours are park operated. Therefore, income is earned from entrance feeds, lodging, food provision, product sales and tours. In the future, licensing of intellectual property, such as logos ad park names, is a possibility. Special promotional co-operation with associated industries, such as 4 by 4 vehicle companies, holds promise. This diverse set of income generators must be further utilized if the SANP is to gain sufficient income to reach the public policy goal of financial self-sufficiency.

Differential fees are becoming more common. Foreigners pay more, and sometimes much more, than nationals do. At high demand times prices corresponding to more services. Those agencies that have parastatal status and have private sector involvement have a much higher diversity of pricing and servicing standards. South Africa is a good example of the development of a wide range of standards and pricing for accommodation in and near the parks. The parks typically provide three levels of basic accommodation services; personal tent camping, RV camping, and semi-permanent tent rentals, the latter of which typically are wood-floored, canvas tents. The parks sometimes also have three different levels of roofed accommodation, ranging form rustic cabins through cottages to hotels. Many parks provide several levels of food provision, from restaurants, through fast food outlets to grocery stores. Merchandise sales are common, typically for typical outdoor gear and souvenirs.

In South Africa the private sector is heavily involved in the upper range market, providing two or three levels of highly priced accommodations and associated ecotourism services at private game reserves. The private reserves are often located adjacent to the parks, to take advantage of the wildlife and ecosystems of the parks as well as the already identified ecotourism profile of the location.

The full range of income generation opportunities in park tourism now being utilized by park agencies are their private sector partners in various locales. A few park agencies are experimenting with the licensing of intellectual property. The names and images of national parks are some of the most well-known and powerful in the world. Private corporations will often pay high sums for the use of these names and images. Cross marketing occurs when one product or organization advertises in concert with another. An example could be a park agency using one type of recreational vehicle, thereby advertising to all the visitors its special qualities in the park environment. In concert, the vehicle manufacturer would publicize the park as the point is made about the special features of a vehicle.

Park Tourism Income Sources

Park Entrance Fees

Recreation Service Fees, Secial Events and Special Services

Concessions

Accommodation

Equipment Rental

Food Sales (Restaurant and Store)

Parking Merchandise Sales (Equipment, Clothing, Souvenirs) Licensing of Intellectual Property

Cross Product Marketing

Parks Canada for the 2000/2001 fiscal year (Parks Canada, 2001). This reveals that this agency relies heavily on three sources of income, entry fees, rental and concessions and camping fees. It also revel as that the agency is not taking advantage of the majority of income sources. For example, lucrative income sources such as food and merchandise sales were not utilized directly. However, some such income would be earned indirectly through concessionaire fees.

Table 7.2: Parks Canada Revenue Sources for 2000/2001

Revenue Source	*Revenue Amount*
Park Entry fees	$30,100,000
Rentals and Concessions	$14,300,000
Camping Fees	$14,900,000
Other Revenue	$6,100,000
Recreation Fees	$4,500,000
Staff Housing	$2,300,000
Interest ad Land Sales	$1,700,000

Australia is a typical example with most park agencies in the country relying on only a few of these sources of income, typically entrance fees some recreation service fees and accommodation fees, usually for camping (Queesland Department of the Environment, 1996). Australia has a long tradition of free public access to natural and cultural heritage assets, so much so that when the Great Barrier

Reef National Marine Park proposed an increase from $1 to $6 for park visitors using commercial tourist operators a Senate parliamentary committee inquiry was launched (Allison, 1998). This inquiry came to the apparently self-evident conclusion that: "It must be accepted that user charges can usually raise no more than a small percentage of total costs." (Allison, 1998, p. 133). This inquiry apparently did not recognize, which is commonly the case, that there are many sources of income that can be obtained from various tourism sources.

In several countries dramatic increases in park use fees were introduced without proper client consultation, most specifically Costa Rica and Zimbabwe, resulting in vociferous objection and subsequent roll-back of some of the increase. The lack of knowledge of pricing policy and the methods of price adjustment is common in parks, and is visibly evident in these two examples.

There are implications for management of higher levels of income based on tourism. Overall, park visitors will face higher fees and more increased opportunity where fees are charged. The biggest changes take place within the park agency. A business approach to management is necessary. This includes the ability to retain and utilized most if not all income. Given the need for income, the park visitors become more important.

Their opinions on programmes, their length of stay, their return rtes, their facility and programme needs and their overall satisfaction become important management variables. The managers become more aware of the need for marketing, that is the creation of a product that fits the market needs. Once the income becomes substantial park management has a higher level of independence from government grants, and from government in general.

Implications of Tourism-based Income

Business-based Management

Increased Profile of Visitors in Management

More emphasis on Client Satisfaction

Service Quality Management

Enhanced Marketing

Independence from government Grants

Higher fees

Experience reveals many resistance factors from the move from a park agency dependent upon government grants, to an agency dependent upon tourism income. Nature is perceived as being universally-owned and requiring no human management. This concept of nature as a free good creates expectations that national parks and other forms of protected areas should provide free access. Over history this concept was reinforced with pricing for access well below the production cost. In the USA national park use fees were prohibited by law for many years. The private sector in tourism usually objects to any fees, and especially to any increase in fees. In addition, it is obvious to many business people in tourism that substantial income can be earned by providing services to park visitors. These people therefore act lie vultures, swooping into the political arena to seize the most important assets, such as accommodation and food provision. This denies the park management from important income sources. Park agencies are typically not equipped to undertake business management. Their marketing, pricing policy, economics and financial expertise are usually deficient. This and other factors lead many park agency staff to vigorously object to a park agency operating as a business. It is common for important sectors of the public, such as environmental groups, to object to the business. It is common for important sectors of the public, such as environmental groups. It can also be due to resistance to paying increased fees.

Resistance Factors to Tourism-based Income

- Public expectation of free nature
- History of pricing below production cost
- Private tourism sector resistance
- Private sector vultures
- Lack of business expertise in agency
- Public concern about commercial development
- Staff resistance to business operation

Tourism Planning and Management Competencies

All national parks and protected areas have some level of visitor use. This can vary from just a few to millions of visitors per year. Much of the visitor managements is reactive, rather than proactive. The parks receive whatever visitor use that occurs, and then try to develop mechanisms to define and manage appropriate activities and levels of use. Often visitor management only takes place when some levels of a problem is perceived. The parks usually provide "take it or leave it levels of tourism service. In other words, a type of recreation programme or facility and a level of service is provided, with the visitor free to accept this, or to not participate. Visitors are expected to make their opinions about activities and services known through management reviews or through complaints, or not at all. It is very rare for park agencies to consistently and professionally evaluate and monitor the wants and levels of satisfaction of their visitors. It is even rarer for evaluation to bed one on potential visitors or past visitors who did not return.

The majority of park agencies are weak in tourism competencies. Those that do occur are usually the result of resource managers learning on the job about visitors and tourism management. Very few agencies, and almost no parks, have professional expertise in leisure pricing policy, in tourism economics, in marketing, in tourism management, in social statistics, in service quality or in leisure studies. However, this situation is changing rapidly in several countries. For example, Parks Canada is one of the leaders in the development of high levels of competency throughout the agency in tourism management. This increase is stimulated by the need of the agency to gain operational income from tourism.

The low level of tourism competency occurs in park agencies where the emphasis on resource protection and the budget comes entirely from a central government pot. However, whenever a park agency starts to move to a tourism-based budget where income from visitor services provides the income, there is a much higher emphasis given to tourism management. Often the private sector operators in and near the parks have much higher levels of tourism market expertise than do the parks. In many parts of the world the private sector I the force behind the tourism in parks. It is the private sector that attracts the visitors, services their basic needs, and provides all of the tourism services. A pointed example of this is in Costa Rica, where the national parks and the wildlife refuges have low tourism competencies within the government agency. It is the private sector that has developed the internationally recognized, park-based ecotourism industry over the last 20 years.

Park Tourism Market

Is there a market for increased levels of nature-based tourism? The largest market study ever undertaken was done for British Colubia and Alberta in Canada in 1995 (HLA and ARA, 1995). For this study, the term ecotourism was used and was defined very broadly as "nature, adventure and cultural experiences in the countryside" (HLA and

ARA, 1995, p. ES-1). The study found a very large ecotourism market in Canada and the United States. In the seven metropolitan areas studied, Seattle, San Francisco, Los Angeles, Dallas, Chicago. Toronto, and Winnipeg a market of 13.2 million potential ecotravellers was found. This was much larger than anticipated, and showed that a large market is now present in North America alone.

The study found that the natural setting is the most critical factor in the determination of a quality product. The tourists showed increasing desire to find experiences in environments that were ecologically well managed. Recreational activities were important and multiple activities were desired. Midrange accommodation was desired, and the experienced ecotourist placed much higher emphasis on the outdoor experience than on the accommodation. Competent guides and quality interpretive programmes enhanced the quality of the travel product experience. The preferred trip was long, at seven days or more. Parks and the activities in the parks were found to be very important components of the ecotravel experience (HLA and ARA, 1995).

Clearly, there is a large and growing ecotourism market in North America. Travel trends throughout the world point to growing markets, especially in North America. Europe and Asia. Given the large potential market size, the key issue becomes one of providing travel products that fit the market and ensuring that these products have positive economic and environmental benefits.

Visitation Statistics

Decisions should be based upon data. The better the data, the better the chance of good decisions. A fundamental figure for decision making is that of product volume. No private company can survive without thorough, accurate and up-to-date data on the numbers and timing of the production and subsequent sale of their products. However, some parks pay low levels of attention to documenting their level of recreation use. In recent years during budget cutting some managers cut gate staff and visitor management personnel, people doing functions seen as less important. Imaging a store firing all its cashiers and its product service personnel!

Many parks are poorly designed for documentation of visitation levels. Parks are often large with many entry points, making it difficult to tablate all entrances. Some park clients sneak in to avoid fees. Many parks do not have staff covering all entrances at all times of the day and all months of they year. Shoulder season visitation is usually poorly documented. Within one agency there may be different data collection procedure sin different parks. And in large parks there may be different data collection procedures at different entrances (Wade, 1998). However, the recent move in Canada and the USA towards parks retaining fee income is reversing this trend and placing much higher emphasis on catching as many of the clients as possible.

Ontario has a history of collecting accurate and useful park use figures, and can be used as an example to illustrate certain points. Figure 1.9 shows the visitation trends in Ontario provincial parks over the last decade, as measured in visitor days of recreation use. Clearly, increases in use continue across the period, shown both in the raw data and in the trend line shown in figure 1.9. It is probable that budget cuts in Ontario throughout the 1990s meant that the figures shown in the last few years are underestimated, as staff are less available to count properly in shoulder seasons and in low-use periods during the days of the heaviest seasons. The dip from 1995 to 1996 is probably due to a large reduction in staff, due to budget cuts. Interestingly the use level increases substantially in the late 1990's even though the fees levels of service, especially for camping

Every park system has its own, unique system of counting and recording its visitors. Some count all who enter, including recreationists, service vehicles, and vehicles just passing though. Some count only those who stay during the night, ignoring day visitors. Some count only those who pay. Some record the numbers of entracts, some the numbers of visitors hours, and others the numbers of visitor days.

There is a need to standriz, in parks, in countries, and globally, the definition, the collection procedures, and the and the reporting of park tourism statistics. When this is done, the park movement will have new and powerful data for influencing public policy discussions.

Recently the World commission on Protected Areas released the first-ever guidelines for the measurement of public use of parks and protected areas (Hornback & Eagles, 1999). This manual provides standardized terminology for park tourism, outlines a five-level system of sophistication for measurement, provides guidance on measurement techniques and technologies, and provides examples of the use of tourism data in park management. The guidelines are intended to assist in the standaridization of park tourism measurement. In 2001 a global abulation of park tourism use levels will be undertaken as part of the preparation of the next edition of the United Nations list of national parks Congress that is to be held in South Africa in September 2003.

Tourism Management Structures

Typically parks are managed by government agencies. In this situation most staff are government employees with a hierarchical form of decision-making. Budgets are provided each year from a central government allocation, with park income being returned to a central government pot. Often visitor services, such as accommodation, tours and consumer products, are provided by concessionaires who are licensed by the agency for a period of time. This model is widespread and reasonably effective when central government provides sufficient budget. However, it is very ineffective in several respects. The budgets are not closely tied to tourism levels, so park management is severely limited in its ability to respond to increase or other changes in visitation levels. Also the park staff recognize that the key people to please are those who provide the budget, such as upper level bureaucrats and politicians. As a result the level of understanding and commitment to park visitors is often very low with this model of management. This model can be problematic when the size and power of the private sector tourism overwhelms apolitically weak government agency. in this situation the selfish individual interests of the tourism operators can lead to tourism overuse. Very severe environmental degradation often occurs with this model, due to the lack of budget for the agency to handle tourism pressures.

Much experimentation with park management structures is underway. Three new models that are having success are worthy of discussion; the parastatal agency, the non-profit. Corporation, and the private, for-profit corporation. Many government agencies are shifting to a parastatal form of operation, as discussed earlier for Cananda. A parastatal is a corporate body within government. The parastatal makes its own policy, maintains internal financial operations, and has control over internal reporting and decision structures. Often a government-appointed Board of Directors functions as the overall policy and approving body, sometimes with veto powers held by a Minister. This approach is in place in Kenya, in Tanzania, in South Africa and in Ontario, Canada, to name four examples. Advantages over the government model are numerous. This structure is much more financially efficient. The agency can quickly establish pricing and tourism policies that enable it to more effectively tap tourism financial flows. The ability to internally handle budgets means a better understanding of the connection between service and income, between outflow and inflow of money. This structure usually leads to much higher levels of emphasis on par visitors, their needs and their satisfaction. This approach often has much flatter structure, with the multiple layers of the government agency replaced by only a couple of administrative layers. The biggest disadvantage of a parastatal, seen by some, is the loss of central control by government.

Those countries with parastatal forms of park agency management are those that are most likely to earn the majority or their entire operational budget from tourism. Examples include Tanzania National parks (TANAPA) in Tanzania, Kenya wildlife Service KWS) in Kenya, and SAN in South Africa. However, it is important to note that in all three of these Africa countries various forms of foreign aid are very important for capital development in the parks.

Some countries utilize non-profit corporations to provide some of the tourism services. These can take the form of membership groups that provide specialized services, such as guiding, information dispersal, and recreation management. Such groups have the advantages of a parastatal plus the additional ability to mobilize large numbers of volunteers and solicit donations. However, this approach is rarely used for entire parks, probably due to the narrow focus of such groups and their lack of ability to handle the entire range of concerns required in park management.

Often for-profit private corporations provide some tourism products and services to visitors in parks. This is frequently done on a licensed concessionaire basis, where the company has a monopoly, or on a free market basis where many companies compete for the tourists market. Occasionally experimentation is occurring where park development or park management is being turned over totally o private companies. One such case is now taking place in Lesotho. The Lesotho Highlands Development Authority is constructing a series of massive dams in the Lesotho highlands, for the purpose of earning income from the export of water to the large urban areas of nearby South Africa. As a remediation effort the Authority has hired a consulting firm to select, plan, design and construct a system of protected areas within the development areas. Four parks are under development, with two, the Bokong Nature Reserve and Tse'hylane National par, at the stage of tourism facility development. At the end of the contract period the private firm will turn over the operational parks to the fledgling national park's agency of the country. This is the only example I have ever seen of a private company given complete authority for the selection, planning, design and construction of protected areas.

Personal observation of the activities suggests that it is a highly effective effort, but the ability of the government park agency to manage the park and the tourism after the hand-over is in doubt. What does it take to effectively manage tourism in a national park or other form of protected area? It might be best to discuss the overall trends in park tourism by summarizing within two heads:

(1) park tourism opportunities and

(2) park tourism challenge.

Spark tourism Opportunities

Within most park agencies the park management authorities have some level of familiarity with park visitation. Most are capable of handling some international tourism. If the parks work within competent, coordinated system and have sufficient finances to operate the parks that exist, it is possible to develop a coordinated tourism management system. For the parks to become international destinations, the country and the parks must have a global image of being a premier destination for outdoor recreation and nature tourism. Potential tourists must see some international profile. Location is important, but poor location can be overcome due to inexpensive air travel. Significant natural resources, a high market profile, and a quality service industry are three prerequisites for effective utilization of the international market.

The international airports, road, and water transportation system must be capable of handling significant levels of tourism traffic. Information systems need to be able to handle the whole range of needs that occur in tourism. People need lots of information. Those sites that have better information technologies are much more effective in attracting international tourism. Unfortunately, most park agencies do not control the flow of the majority of information that is provided to park visitors. Guide books, feature films, conservation groups, scientific publications, and tour companies usually provide more information than do the parks. This can be an advantage if the information is accurate and appropriate, but it can be very problematic if the park is not prepared or capable of handling the resultant tourism traffic. It can also be a probe if the information is wrong, or purposely misleading.

Park Tourism Challenges

Most parks are not now equipped to handle international tourism. Typically these parks lack tourism management capability, sufficient staff, and infrastructure. Examples to illustrate this lack of expertise are easy to find. Many parks do not have the language ability to handle tourism from foreign countries. Often very little is done to encourage and assist visitation by people from foreign countries. Most parks have insufficient numbers of people with expertise in tourism, marketing service quality evaluation, and international ecotourism. The level of expertise in these area must be considerably upgraded if the agencies want to develop a vibrant, international tourism industry, one that an complete globally. Expertise in service quality management this particularly needed. The North American service industries are the global leaders in the development ad application of service quality management principles. As a result, the North American consumer expects high levels of quality from service providers. Government agencies lag far behind the private sector in applying service quality management principles, and this lack is obvious to their clients.

Several countries, most specifically the USA, Australia, and the United Kingdom, have aggressive tourism research, education, and development programmes aimed at nature-based tourism. For example, the National Parks Service of the USA developed a suite of national cooperative research and training institutes at first-line universities in threat country (Michael Soukp, personal communication, November 24, 1997). This follows similar initiatives previously undertaken by the US Forest Service, and another by the US Fish and Wildlife Service. Recently, the park agency in the State of Victoria in Australia funded a major cooperative research and education unit in Deakin University (David eston, personal communication, November 17, 1997; John senior, personal communication, July 24, 1999). The recent nature tourism strategy for the state of New South Wales proposes a strengthened link between the national park agency and universities in hat state of Australia (Worboys, 1997). No such cooperative units are found in most countries in the world. This deficiency results in a severe paucity of professional level of expertise in the specialised area of park tourism. There is an urgent need for the development of better connections between universities and park management. Australia is leading the way with the development of the national research programme for sustainable tourism. This is known as the cooperative Research Centre for Sustainable Tourism (CRC Tourism) and is located in the Gold Coast

Campus of Griffith University (Terry de Lacy, personal communication, July 12, 1999) this operation involves university, government department and private sector cooperation into cutting edge and applied tourism research. This approach appears to be functioning very well with impressive levels of useful tourism research being published.

Many parks are generally unknown outside the local area, and have weak mechanisms to provide a higher level of profile. Man parks have natural resources of limited international appeal. Therefore, it is reasonable to suggest that only some parks can play an international role. Within an overall park system tourism strategy, only those with appropriate natural and managerial resources should be chosen for international visitation.

Only a few parks have an existing international reputation sufficient to attract people to the sites as primary travel destinations. Those that have the name "national par" and "World heritage Site" have significant brand identity. The plethora of park names, such as "provincial park" and "conservation area," leads to confusion by many potential visitors. These names are often poorly known outside the local area. These phrases may also connote low levels of resource significance and tourism infrastructure.

Parks are very important components of the nature-based tourism industry. They occupy some of the most interesting landscapes. They also have information and infrastructure that attract tourists. And they can be used within a system of linked travel routes for long-distance travel. However, the parks are seldom managed within a system of linked travel routes. For example, are the parks part of a clearly-identified travel route? Is all information for all destinations on a route available at all stops along the route? Can a visitor book all accommodation and other services for an entire trip at any of the parks along the route? Typically, the answer to these questions is negative.

Many park administrations show weak understanding of the global ecotourism market. There does not appear to be a policy envelope, an administrative structure, or a staffing complement that recognizes an international role. The big exception to this situation is in Australia, with both national and state-level ecotourism strategies that explicitly deal with the parks as international destinations (Allock, Jones, ane & grant, 1994; Worboys, 1997; Western Australian Tourism commission, 1997; tourism queensland, 1999) The ecotourism policy and plan for the State of queensland in Australia is one of the most mature policy documents available.

An obvious example of the lack of understanding of international tourism is the inadequacy of programmes and facilities aimed in this direction. International visitation is not directed through a well-designed system of information for international visitors. Multilingual publications are almost non-existent. Staff language ability is generally in the local language, often in English, and almost never in other important languages such as German, Spanish, or apanese. Prebook in by international visitors is very difficult or non-existent. There is no way for international tourists to work through their travel agents to facilitate visitation to most parks. Often visitors are expected to bring all the necessary equipment for camping or outdoor recreation, a very difficult and expensive task for trips that involve air travel. Rental or sale of equipment sometimes occurs in the parks, but its availability is spotty, and when available, is difficult to access for international visitors. There is seldom easy access to guides, specialized information, or ethnic food for international travelers. Co-operation with airlines, tour agencies, recreation vehicle rental companies, or hotel chains is rare. Parks do little to encourage, or even facilitate, the visitation by people from the country's major foreign tourism markets. Given these challenges, it is a wonder that as many international travelers find their way to parks as do. It is clear why the Lonely Planet Guides, and other similar guidebooks, have round such a global market. However, if these challenges were tackled effectively by the parks, the numbers of international visitors could increase dramatically.

Often the parks' infrastructure is designed for the knowledgeable and experienced local person. It is difficult for foreigners to visit parks. It is very difficult for them to gain the knowledge of a park, to obtain access, to get all the necessary equipment, to learn how to use the equipment, to gain suitable transport and then to visit most parks. In North America camping is the dominant form of camping in parks. The complexity of camping redirects many visitors into other forms of accommodation. However, there is very limited roofed accommodation in the parks to handle the international ecotourism market. There are often suitable accommodations outside the parks, but these are typically small scale and difficult to access by people in remote locales of the world.

Park tourism is a global phenomenon and has a global market. Those agencies and those parks that develop suitable expertise and facilities are out-competing others. The phenomenal success of national parks and game reserves in South Africa in the last half decade shows how a sophisticated tourism approach can successfully out-compete many other similar destinations in Africa that have equally good natural resources, but less effective tourism operations.

Some of the deficiencies outlined are due to low levels of finance. At present, the typical government agency structure results in insufficient finance to hire trained staff, to develop the research base, to develop the product line, to advertise the product, and to handle the visitors when they arrive. The parastal agency structures developing in many countries help self finance this endeavour when they become operational, but there are often insufficient start-up funds. It is important for governments to recognize that one must spend money to make money. Allocations from governments are necessary for the development of nature-based tourism. These allocations must be made within the context of a carefully constructed national, provincial, and agency policy environment. This aid is often occurring in developing countries through various forms of foreign aid. The global Environment Facility provides grants and soft loans for biodiversity conservation (GEF, 1996) in parks and protected areas, with the long-term operational funds to come from tourism (the World Bank, 1998).

The challenges are partially due to a nature-tourism policy void in many countries. There is an urgent need for coordinated national/provincial/regional nature-based tourism strategies in most countries. These strategies would identify key policy priorities, consider which sites have potential for international ecotourism, develop recommendations for market development, provide backing to financial development, and schedule a multi-year development plan. The Australian national and state nature-tourism policies are the best in the world at the current time (Allockck, Jones, Jane & Grant, 1994; Worboys, 1997, Western Australian Tourism commission, 1997).

If park tourism is to be given the level of public policy recognition that it deserves, a more consistent and thorough procedure for the collection of visitation and economic data is required. Carlson (1997) discussed the complexities of evaluating and monitoring recreation and tourism use. After his study of economic evaluation of recreation and tourism in New South Wales he called for " more consistent approach to data collection." The World Commission on Protected Areas is attempting to standardize the collection and use of park tourism data. Guidelines for the measurement of economic impact of parks are under development (Bagri, Blochhus, & Vorhies, 1998). The goal of this effort is to standardize methods of measurement and encourage the widespread collection and dissemination of the output. Guidelines for the collection and use of visitor-use data (Hornback & Eagles, 1999) are published by the World Commission on Protected Areas. The goals of these two efforts are to standardize the approaches used for economic impact measurement as well s the terminology, the measurement methods, and the reporting of park visitation. These guidelines should be of assistance to all parks agencies.

The next data collection for the United Nations List of National Parks and protected Areas, occurring in the year 2001, asks for visitor-use data from al countries. Once compiled, this inventory will provide the first global documentation of park use. Using economic models, these visitor-use data will be the base for the calculation of global tourism economic impacts.

With the movement toward documentation of tourism's volume and impact, discussion is starting on the evaluation of the park management's ability to handle tourism (Hocking, 1997). The development of management effectiveness guidelines and procedures can assist policy makers senior management, and the public in understanding the capability of park managers and their institutions.

Many parks are starting to move towards agency management structures that function like corporations within government. This involves

(a) agency retention of fee and license revenue,

(b) retention of budget surpluses at the end of the fiscal year,

(c) pricing policies that better reflect the cost of production, and

(d) more flexible arrangements with corporate and non-profit entities outside government. It is probable that higher use fees will be charged. Over time a much higher proportion of revenue will come from merchandise and food sales than now occurs. Innovative funding mechanisms, such as licensing of park names or cooperative public-private ventures in special purpose merchandise, are under way.

Park agencies must develop tourism management competencies within their own organization. It is critical that the park visitors' needs and wants be understood. Most park agencies now function on a take-it or leave-it philosophy towards their visitors. Certain types of facilities and services are provided, and the park client is not even asked if this facility or service is desirable or serving their needs. A class example to illustrate this point is the lack of service quality management in most park agencies. Few agencies have specific service quality goals, with Parks Canada being a notable exception. The private sector in leisure services is rapidly moving towards service quality goal management. All park agencies require specialists in leisure pricing policy. Pricing policy is a major field in business management, and a critical component of the operation of most corporations. Leisure marketing is the specialized field concerned with developing a solid understanding of the client, the product and developing means to match the two. The park agencies with parastatal forms of management are now staffing with specialized expertise in leisure marketing. This paper makes a strong point of the need for tourism and resource economics expertise within a park agency. Those agencies that function like a corporation need specialized finance expertise. Tourism management is a large and specialized field that is a board and complex as resource management. All park agencies should develop staff expertise in this area. It may be too obvious a point to make, but it is important to note that people trained in biology, forestry and resource management typically have no professional training in any of the fields listed. Therefore, it is important for park agencies to retrain their existing staff, or hire such expertise.

The negative impact of tourism on park resources is less influenced by absolute numbers of visitors, and more influenced by weak tourism policy, management and staffing. Very low levels of finance often cause this. It has been shown many times in many parks that with sufficient expertise and finance, park tourism can be very competently managed, with low levels of negative environmental impact and high levels of positive economic impact. The key issue is developing a management framework that emphasizes staff expertise in tourism and financial competence.

CHAPTER EIGHT

International Trends in Nature Tourism

The trends outlined should affect nature tourism management, worldwide, over the next 25 years. This chapter outlines trends in political, social, demographic and technological sectors affecting nature tourism management. Since park finance is ultimately dependent upon larger influences that affect park visitation, tourism, and management, it is important to consider the macro trends that impact on parks.

Trend 1

Growing demands for democratic forms of government translate into increased public participation and collaboration in park planning. Park planning and management developed into professional and bureaucratic forms as parks expanded in size and influence. The limitations of thee approaches started to become obvious as conflicts arose over diverging goals, as strong competitors for resource use arose and as park visitors and local communities became politically active. These influences and the global trends towards more democracy and accountability in government shift park management towards a more open style, with strong public participation and collaboration. Tourism is another pressure towards this approach, forcing park agencies to become more client-focused.

Trend 2

Increased accessibility of sophisticated technology and science means that visitors are knowledgeable about what opportunities exist and the consequences of management actions. Park visitors tend to be well-educated, urbane, well-travelled and open-minded. They are comfortable with advanced science and technology, somewhat strangely considering their strong interest in human-scale technology and human-powered activities in the park. The average park visitor is well aware of the leisure and service opportunities available, both within parks and in other sites. The visitor is aware of and interested in park management, and is capable of forming intelligent positions on a wide range of park management alternatives and actions. This type of clientele is both strongly advantageous to parks, in that they will easily seek out information and opportunities provided by parks, and challe· .ging, as they will aggressively comment upon management actions. These people are sophisticated consumers, with a level of knowledge and savvy that will challenge most park management.

Trend 3

An aging population means the there will be significant demand shifts in what activities, settings and experiences visitors seek from parks areas. Throughout the developed word a revolution is underway in population demography. This area is entering a period with the highest proportion of retired and senior-aged people in history. These people are the healthiest and wealthiest older people in world history. They show strong interest in nature-based activities and travel. They will be a very large potential market for the leisure experiences provided by parks and protected areas. They show strong interest in nature-based activities and travel. They will be a very large potential market for the leisure experiences provided by parks and protected areas. They will not only be consumers of park activities, they may be a large pool of volunteer activity and donations. However, there are challenges. They are not very interested in camping, preferring roofed accommodation. They are less physically capable than younger people. Their ability to travel declines as age-related physical challenges develop.

Trend 4

As educational levels rise, demand for appreciative and learning opportunities associated with parks and protected areas will increase.

In the vast majority of the world, educational levels of the population are rising quickly. There is an increasing participation rate in post secondary education. In the developed world almost 50% of all new jobs involve post secondary education. National park use is highly correlated with higher education levels. Higher education leads to higher service quality demands as well as higher educational service demands. Parks are challenged to provide services and programmes that build on the education trend. However, since higher education levels lead to higher income levels, these people are able to pay for the services that they demand.

Trend 5

In the medium term, advances in the technology of travel and reductions in costs will result in increased demand for park and protected area opportunities distant from one's residence.

For the last 50 years advances in airline technology, energy efficiency, information technology, human social welfare and education led to increases for long distance travel. Such travel affects many parks, and is a critically important export industry for many countries. This trend can be expected to continue in the medium term, for approximately the next 10 years.

For most countries in the world park visitation increased, sometimes dramatically over the last 50 years. This increase can be expected to continue in the medium term.

Trend 6

Continued growing sensitivity to environmental, social, cultural and economic impacts of human activity lead to new and different roles of protected areas, often to multiuse sites similar to biosphere reserves. Private ecolodges and nature reserves develop, funded by tourism.

As parks reach beyond the 10% level of th earth's terrestrial surface, their roles will continue to deepen and diversify. Tourism can adapt to a wide variety of situations. Ranging for low-density wilderness to high density urban and resorts. There is an emerging market for multi-use sites that provide a spectrum of opportunities with in a geographically and conceptually-inked space, such as a biosphere reserve. Such a site can, in one place, provide ranges of experiences dealing with human use density, levels of physical challenge, ranges of accommodation quality and price and levels of interaction with nature from intense to casual.

Private ecolodges are developing strongly in many countries, typically exploiting the market for advanced levels of education and service. These sites vary dramatically in form as the industry experiments with this new type of travel destination. They are already having visibly positive environmental, economic and social impacts in many countries. Many of these sites will challenge pubic parks in the upper scale markets of nature-based tourism.

Trend 7

Growing knowledge about visitors, parks and their interactions lead to more sophisticated and effective methods of managing park-based tourism.

As park tourism continues to develop, as parks recognize

the need to complete for a finite tourism market and as park visitors demand more sophisticated services, park agencies must develop higher levels of tourism management competence. The key areas include:

- Understanding visitors' needs and wants
- Service quality management
- Leisure pricing policy
- Leisure marketing.
- Tourism and resource economics
- Finance
- Tourism management

Trend 8

The global increase in park area, number of parks and park visitation outstrips the capability of many park management institutions.

The ecology imperative is also a cultural imperative in much of the world. As a result societies place increasing amounts of land into parks. However, equivalent amount of money for the effective management of these lands are not forthcoming from taxpayers. Clearly, the new parks, the increasing area to management and the increasing visitation leads to new management challenges. Some of the outcomes of this trend include:

- Financial needs exceeding the current money supply.
- Paper parks.
- Environmental quality degradation.
- Increased emphasis on tourism income,
- Increased use of NGO, volunteer, profit sector management.

Trend 9

Park management shifts gradually from government agency structures, with centralized financial control, to parastatal forms, with financially flexible an entrepreneurial forms of management.

The typical government park agency is designed to make the park visitor into a problem. Such an agency is an expenditure unit with a fixed budget. The agency gets no direct benefit from the visitor and sees the visitor as a drain on that fixed budget. Increases in visitation are problematic with a fixed budget. New areas to manage, increasing numbers of visitors and increasing societal roles for parks all stretch the government agency management model tot eh breaking point.

Government and policy innovators look for alternatives to the government model. Three models come to mind. One is privatizing all of the tourism services to the profit-making sector of society. This brings efficiency, but not necessarily effectiveness and little equity. Another is privatizing many of the tourism services to the non-profit sector, such as Community and Friends Groups. This can provide efficiency, effectiveness and some equity. Another is privatizing within government, the use of the parastatal form of management. The model is increasingly used, often in concept with the non-profit sector. This approach may be the best model to model to provide the most balanced mixture of efficiency, effectiveness, and equity. Examples o park agencies using the parastal model include the park agencies in the following areas:

- Ontario Provincial Parks (Canada's oldest and biggest provincial park system)
- Parks Canada (National parks, National Historic Parks and National Canals)
- TANAPA (Tanzania National Parks)
- SANP (South Africa National Parks)
- Kenya Wildlife Service (Kenya National Parks)

Trend 10

Park management funding increasingly shifts from government grants to park tourism fees and charges. This results in higher levels of visitor focus in management.

It is reasonable to propose that since all people benefit from the ecological and cultural values of parks and protected areas, that all people, through public taxes, should pay for such benefits. However, only park visitors benefit from a trip to a park, and increasingly there is resistance to public funds being spent on such private benefits. Therefore, a substantial portion of park management funding is shifting from taxes to park tourism fees and charges. Parastatal forms of management are particularly effective in handling with this shift. For example, in the 8 ears since Ontario Provincial Parks moved from a government agency to a parastal the agency's cost recovery moved from 32% to 82%. This shift moved the agency more strongly into a client focus, and moved it away from a government hierarchy focus.

Trend 11

Park agencies develop increased sophistication in their understanding and management of park visitation and tourism.

The level of sophistication for park management within park agencies is rapidly increasing. Increasing numbers of visitors and the move to revenue retention stimulate this. Strong innovation occurs in areas such as pricing policy, service quality, accommodation, and food and beverage provision. For example, Krunger National park in South Africa provides many levels of accommodation within the park, 3 in camping and 3 in roofed and lodge accommodation. The private ecolodges on the western side of the park provide 3 more levels, typically at the more exclusive levels. Such innovation allows this nature-tourism industry to capture the maximum level of financial return with this broad range of service provision.

Trend 12

Increasing globalization of information, business and government results in increasing international cooperation amongst park agencies, park visitors and non-governmental organizations.

Globalization affects parks in many ways, two of which will be discussed here: digital convergence and professionalization. Digital convergence results in the rapid, inexpensive and effective global transfer of information. Very soon park managers and park visitors alike will be able to utilize advanced computer power, instaneous access to data bases, Geographical Positioning Systems (GPS) and Geographical Information Systems (GIS) anywhere on the earth's service at any time. The impact on parks can be enormous. For example, a person so equipped could record a bird in the field. Transmit that sound to a central computer that identifies the bird to species, records the location geographically and records the data into a database. Simulta-neously, the visitor may download maps of the site, a summar of all the records of this species and a status report. The activity of wildlife observation becomes profoundly enhanced. Such technology will affect all aspects of park tourism. It is probable that many park visitors will carry such technology with them throughout all areas of the parks they visit.

Park management is vitally important profession that will gain much more influence and recognition as the protector and interpreter of the world's environmental and cultural inheritance. This professionalization will strengthen over time. There will be a much more widespread generation and exchange of knowledge. The World Parks Congress here in Durban is an example of such an exchange. The huge attendance at the Congress is a visible signal of the demand for such knowledge and the many speakers a willingness to share this knowledge. Exchange programmes will flourish as a way of sharing knowledge and professional development. As this field develops, there will be more specialized programmes in park management in colleges and universities. The USA and Canada lead in this area now, but many other countries can be expected to develop such programmes.

Trends 13

Foreign aid and grants from NGOs will increasingly fund biodiversity conservation and sustainable tourism development in developing nations. Increasingly foreign aid and bilateral aid funds biodiversity conservation and sustainable development with the goal of providing both conservation and economic benefit. For example, the GEF Council on October 15, 2002 approved 33 projects worth US $681,000,000. This work programme followed the August 2002 agreement by representatives of 32 governments to contribute US$2.92 billion to fund GEF operations over the next four years.

Often foreign aid provides the capital funding for conservation. Sustainable tourism has the potential of providing o-going conservation and economic benefits.

Trend 14

Increasing demands for resource exploitation, such as oil, gas, minerals, water, and wood, place stronger pressure for the exploitation of park resources. As renewable and non-renewable resources outside parks become scarcer, the demands for exploitation within parks increase. Healthy park tourism provides one counter balance with its politically relevant benefits. However, it is vitally important that these benefits are accurately calculated and effectively communicated.

Trend 15

A substantial number of parks and their tourism will be destroyed by war, famine and civil unrest, especially in Africa and Asia. Some countries will see a decline in park tourism, typically when social unrest is given widespread coverage in the press. Countries with recent tourism declines due to widely-reported social unrest include:

- Zimbabwe (Nature Tourism, both consumptive and appreciative)
- Uganda (Nature Tourism)
- Indonesia 9Cultural and Nature Tourism)
- Israel (Religious Tourism)

Trend 16

International travel will increase until decreasing supplies of inexpensive light oil result in large increases in cost between 2010 and 2020. As the energy costs increase, international travel will decline. Substantial pressure will take place on many parks and protected areas. The world annual oil production will peak some time between 2005 and 2015. This is known as Hubbert's Peak. After this peak, there will be substantial impacts on the global economy and on tourism. Some of the impacts of Hubbert's Peak include:

- Higher energy prices.
- Move from light oil to heavy oil and other energy sources.
- Move to hydrogen economy.
- Lowered long distance travel and international tourism.
- Increased use of urban and near urban parks.
- Energy generation could mean huge financial income for some parks.

Trend 17

Global climate change will affect most parks and most

park tourism. Global climate change will continue to affect many parks. The impacts on park tourism are unclear, however some obvious impacts could include:

- Increasing drying and droughts leading to water stress, droughts and fires.
- Travellers involved with summer outdoor recreation may move into cooler climes to avoid heat stress.
- Substantial changes in snow-based activities with reductions of snow cover.
- Substantial changes in tourism as weather changes typical climate-based recreation seasons (i.e. period of drought, heat and coolness shift).
- Much higher risk exposure with increases in fires, winds and erratic storms.

The next 25 years will see the greatest management challenges ever. Managers must be increasingly skilled at political negotiation, community relations, finance, tourism, and regional ecological management.

CHAPTER NINE

Golobal Economic Impact of Ecotourism

The section on economics examines the current predisposition of researchers to predict the global economic impact of ecotourism, in the addition to a discussion of leakages and the multiplier effect, revenues in parks, and the economic value of land. The section on marketing evaluates the potential of marketing in the ecotourism field, but also addresses the need for such studies to be accurate in their projections of the market, now and in the future. The final section on management issues in ecotourism discusses a number of issues thought to be relevant to the field, including privatisation, not-for-profit organisations and NGOs, agents and operators, and interpretation. The World Tourism Organisation projects that international tourism arrivals will grow from 593 million in 1996 to 702 million by the year 2000, and over 1 billion by 2010. At the same time earnings from international tourism are expected to climb from US$423 billion in 1996 to US$621 billion by 2000, and US$1.5 trillion in 2010 (Luhrman 1997). Such is the magnitude of the tourism industry, which by many accounts is reported to be the world's largest.

With continued growth at the rate identified above he general trend does not appear to be faltering. In a review of the literature on the economic impact of the global ecotourism industry, there is the feeling among some researchers that ecotourism is expanding even faster than the tourism industry as a whole (see Lindberg 1991; McIntosh 1992; Hawkins in Giannecchini 1993), with towards of 20 per cent of the world travel market as ecotourism (Frangialli 1997). Others, however, are more sceptial (Hornman and Beeston in Tisdell 1995) and feel that it is more logical to view ecotourism's growth in a size specific manner than as a general overview. Jenner and Smith (cited in Goodwin 1996) estimate that ecotourism had a global value of $4 billion in 1980, $5 billion in 1985, and $10 billion in 1989. They forecast ecotourism's value to be $ 25 billion in 1995, and $50 billion by the year 2000; whereas Tibbetts (1995-6) illustrates that of the $2 trillion that tourism generates annually, $17.5 billion is from ecotourism, Such statistics indicate the disparate views that exist on the economic impact of ecotourism.

One of the main reasons for such a discrepancy in quantifying ecotourism is the lack of a clear-cut definition of the term (Hawkins in Giannecchini 1993). Foremost in the minds of many local, regional, and national bodies charged with the responsibility of tourism development is the importance of earning money. However, all such regions are not created equal in terms of their ability to generate and keep money within the economy. Simply stated, although tourism will always create an infusion of money into local economies, the amount of money that stays in that economy is subject to a number of factors. In evaluating the impact of money on the economy, economists must understand the multiplier effect and the associated concept of leakage. In general as new money from tourism enters a local economy it changes hands many times, resulting in a cumulative economic impact that is greater than the initial amount of tourist expenditure. This is referred to as the multiplier effect. More specifically, direct income or first-round income is the amount of that spent money that is left over after taxes, profits and wages are paid outside the area and after imparts are purchased (Getz 1990). The money that remains, after these leakages, is referred to as secondary income, which circulates successively through the economy creating indirect income and induced income, again with various amounts of leakage occurring. National multipliers tend to be highest and, according to Bull (1991), have ranged from 2.5 in Canada to 0.8 in Bermuda and the Bahamas. Most of the less developed economies, especially those island economies, tend to be lower because of the high level leakage. It follows that even in the developed world, the multipliers of small towns and countries are typically low (in the neighbourhood of 0.25) because of the higher leakage rates. Leakage rates can be determined by assessing the percentage of money that flows out of the economy. Clearly, those regions or localities that can minimise the amount of money leaving their economy will have more of the initial expenditures left to circulate through the economy.

Those regions or localities that rely upon resources from outside the region or country-human, physical, and monetary—will no doubt suffer by having to pay for their services. The reverse also holds true in that those regions that can sustain a tourism industry based on the resources that they have at hand will potentially be able to prosper under these conditions. This form of leakage is referred to as import substitution. It is an important concept in the context of ecotourism and sustainable tourism because there is much evidence pointing to the fact that tourism, for example in the less developed countries (LDCs), has been hampered by the fact that management control of the industry lies in the hands of external, multinational interests. Hotels, car rental agencies, restaurants, and airlines, all the big money-makers in the tourism industry, are quite often owned by companies that reside outside the destination region, and the destination region relies upon these to export its product through tourism. Tourism is inherently a private-sector activity that capitalises on a market for the purpose of making a profit. A conflict emerges when a profit-motivated enterprise relies on the provision of supply that does not necessarily advocate the same market philosophies.

Parks and protected areas, as public entities, provide the cornerstone for the ecotourism industry. In many cases there is debate over whether parks should be operated more as a business in response to shrinking public budgets. Conventionally the management of parks has *not* been subject to the same market principles and philosophies as the private sector. While it is generally accepted that ecotourism in protected areas has positive economic spin-offs (e.g. direct employment, both on-and off-site, the diversification of the local economy, the earning of foreign exchange, and the improvement to transportation and communication systems), there are also some associated negatives, including the lack of sufficient demand for ecotourism, which could result in the draining of badly needed funds; the fact that ecotourism may not generate local employment opportunities; the fact that leakages may be quite high as they are in many small and developing regions; and the fact that is may not be socially and economically acceptable to charge fees in parks. The preceding discussion alludes to the fact that one of the most significant issues facing parks and protected areas today is the means of attaining funds for their operation—indeed, in many countries, for their survival.

Many parks agencies that have historically relied on certain specific means by which to support their parks and park services have had to consider diversifying in order to maintain good quality programmes and infrastructure. Sherman and Dixon (1991) illustrate five main ways in which to gain revenue from nature tourism. These include:

- *User fees*. These are usually a reflection of the public's willingness to pay, and in recent years have altered into more of a two-tiered or multi-tiered system with a differential scale of fees, the fee varying according to whether the visitor is a resident or a foreigner.
- *Concession fees*. In the case of government, fees are charged to private firms who provide tourists with goods and services (guiding, food, etc.).
- *Royalties*. Souvenier and T-Shirt sales provide a good basis of this type of revenue, which is given to the agency as a percentage of the revenue made on this items.
- *Taxation*. Sales tax, hotel tax, and airport tax examples.
- *Donations*. Tourists can be promoted to contribute money in an attempt to address a local problem (lack of resources or money for endangered species) and, in the process, aid in the management of a protected area.

In the case of the Monteverde Cloud Forest Reserve of Costa Rica, the issue of park entrance fees has been widely discussed in the context of the viability of this reserve. According to Aylward et al. (1996), in the early 1970s visitors, regardless of their origins, were asked to pay a fee of approximately US$2.30 to gain entrance to the reserve. However, owing to the increasing levels of visitation, and the demands placed on the reserve, a new fee structure had to be developed. In 1995 fees were restructured as follows: <$1 for Costa Rica studies: $1.50 for Costa Rican residents; $4 for foreign students; $8 for non-package tour foreigners; and $16 for foreigners on tours (Ibid). Such fees have been instrumental in enabling this private reserve to become more economically self-sufficient.

Tisdell (1995), however, suggests that there are some inherent limitations to the implementation of fees in financing ecotourism developments, including the possibility that few people may visit the site and/or if the park is located in peripheral areas. At alternatives, managers might elect to make visitors purchase permits from park offices, require tourists operators to pay visitor fees (as in the case in many destinations), or erect automatic ticket machines in car parks and trail heads—an approach that has worked well in Pacific Rim National Park, Canada. Laarman and Gregersen (1996) and Steele (1995) concur that pricing holds tremendous power in providing greater efficiency and sustainability in ecotourism, but is seriously neglected in public policy. These authors identify pricing objectives, pricing strategies, and categories of fees in arguing that the user-pays principle and the removal of free access to public lands are perfectly logical today as a means by which to recover costs and, indeed, make money. While it is not necessarily the goal of publicly run natural areas to 'make money', it is for community-run organisations and of course private enterprises. Laarman and Gregersen offer some guiding principles for fee policies in nature-based tourism.

Laarman and Gregersen argue that pricing objectives can by many-sided, and administrators are constantly challenged to set fees in accordance with the resource conditions of the park, the needs of the park staff, and the needs of visitors. The guiding principles are varied and range from a relationship of fees to general sources of revenue, fees for certain sites, fees only for certain sites, and the management an accounting of fee system. In some park systems fees that are generated in each of the individual parks go back into a general operational account. The positive spin-off of this is that the money that is generated for this account aids in the maintenance of parks in the entire system. The negative element is that those parks doing the best job (either because they have better administrators or because the park simply generates more visitation) do not get the opportunity to utilise directly for their own purposes, the money that they generate. This type of fee philosophy may further decrease the motivation of those working in the money-generating parks, so that they become less conscientious, and may lead those in the money-losing parks chronically to rely on the money generated in other areas.

Steele (1995) illustrates that a policy allowing for open accessibility to ecoturism sites leads to certain economic a ecological inefficiencies. Economic inefficiencies occur in the sense that if sites allow free entry they lose the rental value of the resource. Agencies must also be wary to excess demand where sites are left vacant during certain seasons of the year, and also of costs related to congestion where tourists impact on each other owing to overcrowing (congestion costs are found tc reduce the profit per tourist by lowering tourist demand and raising marginal costs for the supplier). Ecological inefficiencies include consideration of carrying capacities and an analysis of the total volume of tourists and the damage done per tourist. By distributing tourists appropriately in space and time, some natural areas, according to Steele, have been able to increase the numbers to the natural area and reduce the overall impact of these tourists. Also of importance to Steele is the choices than land managers have with respect to pricing controls and quality controls (limits on numbers of users, which are employed more often than pricing controls). This author suggests that the use of variable tariffs or tiered pricing is an efficient way to increase revenue (see the example of Monteverde, above), where foreigners are charged a higher entrance free than locals. The most oft-quoted example of this is the Galapagos Islands, where foreign tourists are charged the equivalent of US$40 and local tourists US$6.

McFarlane and Boxall (1996) write that, historically, many public wildlife agencies get their funds from hunting and fishing licences and general tax revenues. However, owing to the recent decline in many consumptive forms of outdoor recreation (e.g. hunting), and budgets, financial resources for conservation initiatives are dwindling. Their research of 787 birdwatchers indicated that this group shows great promise in supporting conservation efforts in a number of ways. While committed and experienced birders could help to identify wildlife management issues and participate in fieldwork with various agencies, the less specialised birders could aid by improving birds habitat in their backyards and through the contribution of funds. The research demonstrates that conservation agencies must diversify and include innovative schemes to capture the interest and support of the birding population.

The Value of Land

In determining the appropriate use of a resource area, government and other decision-makers must determine the most financially and socially acceptable use of the land. Decisions must be made whether or not (and how) to develop land such as dams, parks, and protected areas, mining, or forestry, all of which have certain associated costs and benefits which will most certainly differ in different settings. Land planners and developers have begun to recognise that destinations are increasingly demanding business ventures that will add value to raw materials (McIntosh 1992); Theophil 1995), instead of taking it away. While many of the large tourism developments of the 1950s, 1960s, and 1970s occurred with only the financial motivations in mind, these days, inmost cases, such large endeavours are undertaken with both ecological and socio-cultural impacts in mind. Given ecotourism's attractiveness as a sustainable tourism option, it is critical to have development ideas accompanied by appropriate social and ecological measures. One of the most effective ways in which to decide on how best to develop or not develop an area of land is through the implementation of a cost-benefit analysis, which includes easily quantifiable costs and benefits (such as start-up and operating costs) and those which are not easily quantified, such as impact assessments. Despite the difficulty in doing so, researchers have endeavoured to place values on ecological and social settings and situations.

In the case of the environment, Munasinghe (1994) has categorised economic values attributed to ecological resources by examining the use and non-use values of assets. In the figure, Munainghe shaded the option values (an individual's willingness to pay for the option of preserving the asset for future use), the bequest values (the value that people derived from knowing that other people will benefit from the resource in the future), and the existence values (the perceived value of the asset) as a caution to the fact that they are all quite difficult to define. From here, analysts may use a number of non-market valuation techniques to quantify the above values (Munasinghe 1994; see also De Lacy and Lockwood 1992), including the travel cost method and the contingent valuation method.

The travel cost method, for example, has been employed by Menkhaus and Lober (1996) in Costa Rica as a means by which to estimate the values of ecotourism to tropical rainforests, based on a sample, of US Travellers. This valuation method, according to the authors, 'estimates ecotourism benefits of a protected area based upon observed travel expenses by visitors to an area' (*ibid.:* 2). These estimates are then used by decision-makers to address issues related to entrance fees, competing land uses, and so on. The argument for the use of such a method is that certain goods such as parks, are not effectively valued on the basis of entrance fees alone; individuals, it is felt, would be willing to pay much more to experience the good. The measure of the value of a good such as ecotourism to a protected area is represented by the consumer surplus. In their study Menkhaus and Lober estimated the consumer surplus to be approximately $1,150, which represents the average annual per person valuation of the ecotourism value of protected areas in Costa Rica for the sample. These authors estimated the annual ecotourism value to Costa Rica's rainforests by this population at $68 million, which is determined by multiplying overall US ecotourists visitation to Costa Rica by the per person consumer surplus.

An example of the contingent valuation method is found in the work of Echeverria et al. (1995) in their evaluation of the Monteverde Cloud Forest Reserve of Costa Rica. This technique, otherwise known as the direct or survey method, is an approach 'in which individuals are asked directly about their willingness to pay for some improvement in a resource or for additional use of a resource' (Smith 1990b: 249). This can take the form of an assessment of the willingness of tourists to pay for habitat protection. Echeverria et al. sought to address these non-market values of the visitors to monteverde in demonstrating that, on average, foreigners were willing to pay $118 of their own income to secure reserves such as Monteverde. This figure is comparable to the willingness of British Columbia residents to pay money to increase the scope of the protected areas in that province.

In valuing places like parks and protected areas (and tourism within such areas), it must be realised that there is a significant degree of grey area between the ideologies of business and those of conservation. Profit and preservation, therefore, are often construed as a partnership, according to Carey (in Giannecchini 1993), that is analogues to an arranged marriage, not one based on love. For example, Giannecchini notes that:

Their [the tourism industry's] customary goal of quick optimum profits is in direct conflict with long-range goals of protection and conservation. This does not mean that the only, or even primary, relationship between the tourism industry and conservationists must be adversarial. But it does mean that whatever laudable, environmentally sound policies and goals the industry articulates, they will remain subsidiary to the demand for profit. Therefore, if the tourism industry becomes the principle force in the development of ecotourism, it will almost certainly be detrimental to long-range environmental concerns.

A key means by which to prove the value of ecotourism (in economic terms) to those advocating other land uses has been economics. Researchers have looked at this type of tourism as a means by which to demonstrate that in light of other competing types of land use, ecotourism presents itself as an effective form of land use. For example, McNeely (1988) estimated the economic worth of specific animal species in Amboseli National Park in Africa. The figured that each lion is worth about $27,000 per year, and each elephant herd at $610,000 per year, which far exceeded the amount of money that could be gained through hunting these animals. Western and Thresher (1973) wrote that in Amboseli tourism could be much more environmentally desirable than agriculture, and in addition earn vastly more per unit hectare of land ($40 per hectare from tourism and $0.80 per hectare from agriculture).

This form of analysis brings to mind the ways in which people value objects such as wildlife. Clearly these is the economic focus, yet examples of this to some degree are required as a means by which to rationalise the existence or occupance of something, like ecotourism as a new land use. Kellert (1987) suggests that attitudes towards wildlife as a commodity or utilitarian object became less widespread in American society between 1900 and 1975. He believes, however, that this attitude change has occurred in only some parts of society. Those who are elderly, rural, in a lower socio-economic category, and who live and work in resource-dependent occupations still harbour negative perceptions of wildlife. It is often difficult for those who are not in one of the aforementioned categories to conceive of such perceptions. Although the point is not made in Kellert's research, one wonders about the impact that urbanisation, education, and wealth have in shaping the more positive attitudes towards wildlife. Ecotourism is, or has been conventionally considered an activity pursued by those who are better educated and wealthier than the 'average tourists', which would, according to the work of Kellert, lead one to believe that these individuals have a better chance of appreciating wildlife. Those who are providers of the ecotourism experience in the least developed countries—assuming that they are not part of the privileged elite of that country-must acquire a 'personal conviction that land managed for wildlife is land ultimately more satisfying, attractive and enjoyable for people' (Kellert 1987: 228).

Marketing

Mahoney (1988) has suggested that tourism marketing fundamentally differs from the marketing of other types of products in three important ways;

(a) tourism is primarily a service industry, where services are intangible, and quality control and evaluation of experiences are more difficulty to envision;

(b) instead of moving the product to the customer, the customer must travel to the product or resource; and

(c) people usually participate in and visit more than one activity and facility while travelling. Therefore, tourism-related businesses and organisations need to cooperate to package and promote the tourism opportunities available in their areas.

The marketing of tourism products in strongly based on a firm understanding of the fact that the overall travel market is partitioned into selected market segments. Travel firms do not have the resources to tap the overall travel market, nor the inclination, owing to the magnitude of domestic and international travel. Instead, business target certain segments based on the product that they are selling and the needs and expectations of the group to which they wish to sell. Target marketing can occur in four main ways;

(1) geographically, on the basis of geographical space;

(2) demographically, based on age, gender, religion, race, etc.:

(3) psychographically, based on individuals' lifestyles, attitudes, values, and personalities; and (4) benefits, which include an analysis of the benefits sought by tourists and the costs they avoid.

Marketers typically follow a systematic planning approach that enables them to focus on their organisational goals, and the specific needs to their clientele in association with various tourism products. A typical plan, based on the work of Lovelock and Weinberg (1984), is outlined. The first stage of the marketing plan involves the identification of the direction of the agency or organisation and the associated priorities that must be followed. This is followed by the definition of markets that will allow the organisation to achieve its chosen goals. Upon the completion of this stage, the organisation endeavours to examine fully the behaviour, needs, and characteristics of the market. Once the markets have been segmented, the organisation can develop specific strategies which must be tailored to each segment. There follows the implementation of a monitoring and evaluation component, with subsequent modification in the future.

Demand is very much an integral part of the relationship between the tourism product and the market, and hence

Krippendorf (1987) feels that in the future tourism marketers must be more sensitive to the changing composition of the tourist population. He suggests that owing to the changing lifestyles, economic conditions, and demographic structure of travellers, 'the market is shifting from manipulated, uncritical "old tourists" to mature, critical and emancipated "new tourists" (*ibid.*: 175). Eleven years on, this trend has certainly taken shape.

As is the case with the conventional travel markets, marketing research in the area of ecotoruism has begun to flourish. The work of Ingram and Durst (1987) stands out as one of the earliest studies in this area, through their development of a bibliography on marketing nature oriented travel in the developing countries, and a subsequent publication that looked specifically at promotion of nature tourism in developing countries (Durst and Ingram 1988). From their research they concluded that there was a need to improve the operations of tourism offices in the developing world. They also found that although marketing is common in the developing world, countries that are to promoting their natural attractions are likely to miss the opportunity to capitalise on the growing ecotourism market.

Ryel and Grasse (1991) suggest that the two cornerstones to effective marketing in ecotourism are the attraction for tourists (which includes biodiversity, unique grography, and cultural history), and tourism infrastructure to support the industry. Given these criteria, agencies are free to undertake the necessary marketing requirements to attract tourists. These authors imply that it is important to attract or market to the 'right' clientele. This includes 'born' ecolourists (those who have a built-in predisposition towards nature and nature travel), and 'made' ecotourists, who can be identified as representing latent demand of those who are unfamiliar with this form of tourism but who can be attracted through effective marketing. Ryle and Grasse suggest that a basic approach to marketing the ecotourism product is through (1) the identification of the characteristics of a desired group, (2) appropriate advertising, (3) careful crafting of the advertising message, and (4) the development of a mailing-list. These authors further suggest that there is a definitive need to classify ecotourists on the basis of demographic, psychographic, and geographical variables, for, as Mayo (1975) has suggested, demographics alone are not an effective means by which to segment the market. This fact has been further identified by Silverberg *et al.* (1996), who undertook an investigation into the psycholographics of nature-based travellers. After identifying six factor dimensions on the basis of the their survey of 334 travellers to the southeastern United States (education/history, camping/tenting, socialising, relaxation, viewing nature, information), they concluded that psychographic research is an effective way for marketers to understand the nature-based traveller better. In Australia, the Office of National Tourism undertook a market study of ecotourists in an attempt to understand the ecotourists market better and target ecotourism products more effectively (Commonwealth of Australia 1997).

This research involved a number of focus groups involving ecotourists (actual and potential) from across the country. In general, the study found that ecotourists are seeking the following;

(a) areas/attractions of natural beauty;

(b) small groups away from crowds;

(c) some level of interaction with the environment;

(d) interaction with like-minded people (see also Fennell and Eagles (1990);

(e) some degree of information and learning; and

(f) fun and enjoyment. More specifically, the research uncovered three broad ecotourism market segments.

These are as follows:

Impulse. Characterised by nature-based day trips away from the main tourist destinations and mainly booked locally by both domestic and international tourists. The level of activity on these tours varies widely.

Active. Characterised by younger and middle-aged professionals who generally book in advance. There is a skew to domestic tourists, although there could well be potential for grown through international marketing, infrastructure, and product development.

Personalised. Essentially older professionals (or retired) who expect to be well looked after by the operator. This segment is skewed to international tourists who book overnight ecotours before arriving in Australia (Commonwealth of Australia 1997: 4-5).

In 1994, the Canadian provinces of Alberata and British Columbia published a comprehensive marketing study (ARA Consultants 1994) which focused on assessing current and future demand for ecotourism in these regions. The authors of the report sought information from a variety of sources in formulating their study, including a literature review of ecotourism, at travel trade survey, a general consumer survey of the residents of seven major metropolitan cities in Canada and the United States, and a survey of experienced North American ecotourists. Ecotourists was defined as "vacations where the traveller would experience nature, adventure, or cultural experiences in the countryside' and hence treated cultural tourism, adventure tourism, and ecotourism as being synonymous. One of the main conclusions from this research was that 'the ecotourism market is definitely expanding to encompass not only those with specialist skills seeking strenuous adventure, but also clients seeking activities supported by amenities, a higher level of services, and requiring lower levels of specialist skill'. This finding is no doubt a result of the methodology employed in the study. Other conclusions of the study are as follows: For the general consumer group, 77 per cenf said they had an ecotourism vacation, with the remaining 23 pr cent expressing interest in ecotourism travel. This led the researchers to conclude that from the general consumers of the seven cities surveyed, the actual market ranges from 1.6 to 3.2 million visitors, and the potential market is approximately 13.2 million ecotravellers. To two of Canada's most beautiful and 'natural' provinces, it is not inconceivable that travellers would involve themselves in any type of natural, adventure, or cultural experience. This probably extends to hard-path ecotourism trips .right along the spectrum to bus tours of the city of Victoria.

The point to be made from this example is that researchers and practioners must proceed cautiously in making inferences on the size and scope of the ecotourism market. Past research has concluded that ecotourism is a very small part of the overall tourism continuum. Although it is certainly growing, so are the ways in which to classify and define ecotourism, many of which are based on convenience and less on a thorough review of ecotourism and ecotourism types. Thus the main fault of the research lies in the fact that it makes the assumption that, apart from the involvement of cultural and adventure tourism types, experienced and inexperienced ecotourists are one and the same. In substantiating this point, Wight (1996:3) reports that, with respect to the experienced North American ecotourists sample.

Because client lists were volunteered, it is not known to what degree those firms volunteering names are representative of the ectourism travel trade. Consequently, it is also not known how representative the respondents are of all ecotourists. However, the sample does represent a large number of experienced North American ecotoruism travellers. In this case the softest of the soft-path ecotourists (or culture and adventure tourists) are grouped with the hardest of the hard-path ecotourists, groups which are perhaps worlds apart in their attitudes, motivations and benefits sought. This ambiguity is indicative of the activity packages offered by the tour operators from which the 'experienced ecotoruism' sample was drawn. Ranked in order of number of packages offered, hiking was first, followed by rafting, canoeing, cycling, Kayaking, horseback riding, and then wildlife viewing-activities which are more skill oriented and less learning oriented in nature. Consequently, it was found that water-based activities were important, but particularly important to the experienced ecotourists (not surprising, and due most likely to the types of ecotourism packages offered); virtually all ages of adults are interested in ecotourism; and interest in ecotourism is spreading to less educated groups.

The results of this study have an element of inclusiveness, indicative of the rather loose methodology employed. Accordingly, the usage of the term 'ecotourism' has spun out of proportion and been misused as an industry label to capture a larger percentage of the travel market (see Goodwin 1995), with the main implication of misrepresenting of 'watering down' the ecotourism market. For example, Thompson (1995) writes that a cruise abroad luxury liners, scuba diving, and helicopter sightseeing trips over Hollywood are all being touted as ecotourism. Clearly, in such cases ecotourism has been modified, repackaged, and 'mass' produced to the point where the line between what ecotorusm is and is not, is quite blurred. If this is the approach by the industry, and if ecotoruism is to become successful by conventional industry standards, it will have undermined exactly what it set out to accomplish in the first place. Referred to as colabelling, this issue has been the source of recent debate over the TRINET (the tourism research international computer link organised out of Hawaii). For example.

When I sought to 'dive with the seals' in Kaikoura

NZ I was attracted to a nice glossy brochure with eco-labelling. My accommodation host saw my interest and recommended another company, a fellow who 'started it here'. When I met the fellow with this beat-up four wheeler hauling his van of live gear I was wondering if I made the right choice. I had a great time and discovered later that the company with the glossy brochure had been in trouble with the Dept of Conservation for exceeding their permits and was told that they would take 24 people out with 12 permits and put half of them in the water at one time.

Ryan (1997) follows up on this discussion by making similar observations on the state of affairs in New Zealand. He suggests that there are basically two types of ecotour operators: one that constructs a glossy pseudo front and the other that is small in scale and that happily accepts size restrictions. Continuing the discussion, Oppermann (1997) felt that too many tourists are subsumed under the ecotourism label—a stance adopted in this book—and that researchers need to be wary of studies that use wide-ranging definition of the term. In order to avoid the misrepresentation of the ecotourism 'industry', Mason (1997) suggests that a system based on self-regulation is suspect and fraught with abuse. He would rather see a form of policing and/or monitoring to avoid the unacceptable behaviour of those operating under free-market conditions. The problem to many marketers, operators, and agents has become so bad that they are refusing to use the ecotourism label because it has gained a poor image and means very different things to different people (Preece et al. 1995).

A further problem for regions in the development and marketing of an ecotourism product is the fact that there seems to be a feeling of unlimited assurance that ecotourism will ultimately resolve any tourism dysfunctions within a region. Tourism decision-makers and planners, perhaps on the basis of overly optimistic forecasts of management consultants, often inherently believe that their jurisdictions will be competitive in a highly competitive global ecotourism market. This has currently become as issue in Canada, where provinces that cannot hope to compete at the scale of other provinces—owing to their geological and natural features—have unbridled optimism for the sector. There is no question that ecotourism can and will exist in these regions, but regions must be realistic about the success of ecotourism initiatives. The size and extent of the sector will be a function of the demand, but it does not restrict them from creating innovative schemes to attract ecotourists given the attraction base from which they have to work.

As a case in point, the province of Saskatchewan, in association with Industry Canada, has recently commissioned as study on the market potential of ecotourism in the province (Anderson/Fast 1996a, b). The research was designed to gather valuable information from the travel trade (companies currently operating adventure, culture, nature, and ecotour trips) on the potential for Saskatchewan as an ecotourism destination. One of the survey questions sought industry response on nine potential ecotour packages to be offered in the province. In only one case did over 50 per cent of the tour companies sampled feel that they could sell the package to their clients. One of the most significant ecotour attractions in the province is the migratory and resident bird populations. However, in the case of the 'Birding in Saskatchewan' tour, only 43 per cent of the operators said that this tour appealed to them, and only 48 per cent said they could sell the package to their clients. The reasons cited for the lack of interest included 'wrong fit' 'too expensive.' And 'not stunning enough'. Other findings of the study indicated that a lack of information on the province and lack of demand for Saskatchewan ecotourism products were two most frequently cited barriers confronting the ecotourism industry in Saskatchewan.

A report on the ecotourism opportunities for Hawaii's tourism industry (Centre for Tourism Policy Studies 1994) put ecotourism and Hawaii into perspective by acknowledging the fact that Hawaii faces some stiff competition from already well-established global ecotourism destinations (i.e. Latin America, Africa, and Asia). They found that the main consideration constraining ecotoruism in Hawaii could be summarised as follow (pp. ii, iii):

1. *Hawaiis physical characteristics.* Hawaii's isolation, limited size, and fragile natural environments create conditions which can lead to irreversible environmental harm from the overuse of its nature resources.

2. *Hawaii's culture and local lifestyle.* Native Hawaiian issues and the preservation of community values have become increasingly sensitive to land use decision-making.

3. *Hawaii's competition abroad.* Hawaii faces competition from a number of well-established ecotourism destinations including countries in Central and Latin America, Africa, Asia, and the Pacific. Island destination areas include the Caribbean, Mexico, the Galapagos, and the South Pacific.

4. *Hawaii's dependence on a mass tourism economy.* Ecotourism's contribution to Hawaii's economy will be modest in comparison to Hawaii's mass tourism industry and should be viewed in terms of diversification, not substitution.

5. *Hawaii's popular image.* As an ecotourists destination, Hawaii will have to overcome its sun, sand, and surf reputation and the impression that it is too overdeveloped to appeal to outdoor enthusiasts seeking back-to-nature experiences.

6. *Private-sector investment.* Owing to the relatively low return/high-risk nature of the ecotourism industry, venture capital and investment support for small business enterprise development are limited while

liability costs (i.e. insurance) for landowners remain high.

7. *Public policy consideration.* There is presently a lack of policy which formally addresses ecotourism issues, resulting in inadequate support for the development and maintenance of ecotourism resources.

These barriers nicely encapsulate the constraints that Hawaii will probably encounter in its planning and delivery of ecotourism is the state. Other regions should be equally wary in the development of their ecotourism product. Substantiating ecotourism through inaccurate research methods is as disruptive as the development of an ecotourism industry on the basis of other related, and less ecologically sensitive, forms of tourism.

Privatization of Ecotourism Management Issues

The idea behind the partnering of public and private sectors is not a new one. Adams (1983) reports that in the realm of community development, such endeavours came into being during the early 1970s. He further illustrates that a number of trends have emerged that help define the scope of such public-private interactions, which include the fact that:

1. Local governments are becoming increasingly concerned with maximising efficiency through improving management and streamlining service systems.
2. New ways of leveraging existing public resources are being explored.
3. Local governments are beginning to alter their delivery systems to use existing resources in new ways.
4. Cities and countries increasingly are having to consider almost completely devolving certain responsibilities back to citizens.

In general, privatisation, in the sense used here, refers to an arrangement entered into by an employer and an outside firm whereby production or service work which was or could have been done by their own employees and equipment is to be performed by the outside firm (Young 1964). Privatisation is, in most cases, synonymous with the contracting out of services, but emphasises the *private sector's* role in fulfilling or winning these contracts (it is important to note that contracts may also be given to those in the not-for-profit sector). Similar in nature to the aforementioned definition is one by Courchene (cited in Beres 1986) who wrote that privation is the private provision of a publicly financed service; while Heald (1984) suggests that privatisation is the strengthening of the market at the expense of the state.

As a result of the increasing pressure on governments to be more accountable with fewer resources, and in the absence of any change in this trend in the foreseeable future, public service providers are caught in the dilemma of how best in the light of the changing socio-economic conditions, to accomplish traditional goals such as service provision and accessibility. Given these changes, it is safe to say that in all probability there are few communities that have not endeavoured to privatise in one way or another. This assertion is best summed up by Beres (1986: 4), who illustrates that good managers have always looked to the private sector when it did not make sense to employ people on a full-time basis.

In an extensive overview of the topic of recreation policy in Canada from the municipal perspective, Smale and Reid (1995) suggested that the decision to privatise, or not, is really a reflection of the perceptions and interpretations of what is a public good. On the one hand, these authors feel that partnerships with the volunteer and private sectors may be necessary in order to deliver as much as possible to the entire community. On the other hand, they felt that in the debate on privatisation, policy-makers must consider what they value in providing for the community: privatisation may be interpreted as a public good in today's ideological world which places an emphasis on the *profitability* rather than the *accessibility* of leisure opportunities. If the service can be provided through the market place, then it may very well end up there without great concern for its value as a public good. Consequently, even though the service may become 'successful', it would likely only serve a certain segment of the population, and hence, would no longer be available to the entire community; in other words, the principle of equal opportunity would be compromised.

Mintzberg (1996) is a firm believer in the notion that capitalism driven by the private sector is throwing the societies of the Western world out of balance. He would rather see a move to the incorporation of normative control, or values, beliefs, and human dedication in the provision of goods and services (the Japanese have been successful using this approach). He continues by suggesting that 'we all value private goods, but they are worthless without public goods—such as policing and economic policies-to protect them' (p.117). Mintzberg substantiates his claim by referencing the current preoccupation with privatisation of public services in today's economy. He suggests that in some cases privatisation is warranted, but in most other cases we are too prone to scrutinizing what does not belong in government when we should be equally diligent in assessing what does not belong in the realm of private business.

In areas more central to tourism, privatisation has generated much debate in the realm of destination promotion at the state and national levels. Bonham and Mak (1996) provide a good overview of the history of private and public financing of Hawaii as a destination, which they use to put the private/public promotion debate into context:

Faced with growing voter opposition to pubic financing of tourism promotion, governments are increasingly asking the tourist industry to assume a larger share of the burden of financing destination promotion. However, asking the industry to make greater voluntary contributions will not succeed without some form of government intervention. Because destination promotion is a public good, individual beneficiaries have the incentive not to contribute and instead to free-ride on the contribution of others.

From a philosophical standpoint, there needs to be some clarity established in better understanding the role that privatisation could play in developing and less developed countries, and in the mass tourism and the ecotourism industries. For example, Jenkins (1994) has illustrated that privatisation will become more prevalent in the Third World as a pragmatic sift in policy-slowly overtime. He further acknowledges that such commercialisation would enable the industry to become more sensitive to market trends and forces. The private sector's role is one that is concerned with profitability. When ecotourism is involved caution must be employed from a marketing perspective for the simple reason that preservation of ecosystems and just social and economic practices may be compromised in an all-out assault on profit. Tisdell (1995) writes that investment in ecoturism takes the form of private firms and public agencies intent of making a profit or surplus from the development of ecotourism. In the case of the public agencies, investment usually occurs in an attempt:

(a) to make a profit or surplus from ecotourism to supplement its funds for conservation managment;

(b) to add to political support for the conservation body, or avert political hostility or lack of political support; and

(c) to improve the working conditions and salaries of employees.

Eagles (1995) feels that private reserves have a role to play in the provision of ecotourism services in Canada. Notwithstanding, he feels that parks services (*i.e.* Ontario Provincial Parks and Parks Canada) should be flexible enough to do a better job at financing their parks. He cites the fact that such parks will be ill prepared to accommodate visitation in the future as they increase in number with continued decreases in funding. Eagles feels that in order for parks to be more business-like, they will have to look closely at revenue retention, willingness to pay, and fees for service as means by which to balance their books, visitor satisfaction, and resource protection.

In a review of ecotourism, less developed countries and parks and protected areas, Fowkes and Fowkes (1991) identify four different goods in relationship to the element of privatisation. They feel that both common goods, such as air, rain, and fish (individually consumed, and difficulty to control), and collective or jointly consumed goods, such as national health services, should not be privatised. On the other hand, toll goods (e.g. telephone systems) and private goods (e.g. foodstuffs), where consumption can be controlled by the supplier, ought to be in private hands. These authors feel that parks and protected interests. It is only when toll goods and private goods (accommodation) are provided in parks that privatisation should be considered as a strong option. In most cases involving support services e.g. computers), retail activities (e.g. restaurants), tourist buildings, and infrastructure (e.g. roads), private intervention should be considered from the perspective of management, maintenance, control of access, marketing, and construction. Private involvement in aspects of the land or those that inhabit the land (plants and animals) is not appropriate.

No Profit Organisations

Depending on the perspective from which one approaches the concept and delivery of ecotourism, there may or may not be a natural linkage between ecotourism and the not-for-profit sector. In many cases the link that does exist between the two (parks and not-for-profits) is based on the vested interest in how such parks should be preserved in the face of competing usage. Although one should not assume that not-for-profit organisations with environmental mandates are not conscious of the value of money in the administration of their operations, their motives can be thought of as being more part-or education-or ecology-centred than profit-centred when compared to the private sector. While not-for-profit agencies are typically bound by the demands of a board of directors whose responsibility is to effectively direct programme and operational policy and decision-making within the agency, earnings that are made beyond operational costs (including salaries) are poured back into the programmes, rather than into the pockets of management/employees.

Gardner (1993: 19) illustrates that an environmental non-government organisation (ENGO) is a citizens' group whose activities include efforts for environmental conservation. Generally these coalitions have the following characteristics; (1) voluntary membership in the group; (2) the group is not profit motivated; (3) it is autonomous, in that it makes its own decisions; (4) it is service driven; and (5) it seek change on behalf of its membership, society, and the environment. However, NGOs are simply defined as 'not government,' and can take the form of not-for-profit status or profit status. There appears to be an interesting dilemma evolving on this front.

In a recent survey of US-based nature tour companies, Higgins (1996) illustrated that the not for-profit sector has a firm stake in the delivery of ecotourism opportunities. Eleven tour operators (17 per cent of the samply total) were not-for-profit, serving some 20,215 clients. Forty—two per cent of their client trips were offered in North

America, which compared to 7 per cent of the rest of the sample, which were commercial in nature. Also, it was suggested by Higgins that the not-for-profit sector was quite active in securing its share of the market by using 'sophisticated marketing campaigns, including direct mail, advertising in tourism publications, and the development of glossy nature-tour brochures' (Higgins 1996: 16) In other research, Weiler (1993) found that on the basis of a content analysis of 55 tour operators' brochures involving 402 tour descriptions, 336 were private-sector tours and 66 were not-for-profit or university-run tours. Universities are given the status of not-for-profit, yet they sponsored and ran programmes designed to make money.

The jury appears to be still out on the relationships between the not-for-profit agencies in ecotourism. One of the main issues related to the profit and not-for-profit sectors in the quality of the tours that they run. Although no data were found in order to elaborate the point, it is nevertheless an issue of great concern for ecotourists and members of host communities. Given ecotourism's local development mandate one could argue that the not-for-profit agencies (all things considered equal) would be the more legitimate tour operators. This is supported by Ziffer (1989), who feels that the not-for-profit sector is a small but growing segment of the ecotourism industry with plenty of potential in establishing appropriate ecotourism development models for the future.

Agents and Operators

Travel agents and tour operators are key stakeholders in the relationship that exists between the destination and the tourist. Both have a tremendous influence on tourists relative to the choices made and types of experiences gained for travel. To destinations eager to capture part of the tourism market, agents, although not the only means by which travellers learn about various destinations must be familiar with the broad spectrum of opportunities available to the travelling public. Milne and Grekin (1992) and Wilkinson (1991) report that at least for some peripheral destinations, or those just starting to develop a tourism product, travel agents can play a critical role in counselling 'destination-naïve' tourists. The information profile of destination-how firmly entrenched it is as a travel option-especially to the travel agent, therefore, places each destination in a position of competitive advantages or disadvantage.

Tourism opportunities have historically been offered through operators, whom Metelka (1990: 110) defined as owners or managers of a place of business. Recent evolution in the terminology has included the 'outfitter', which is representative of the fact that ecotourism is spilling over into the realm of the outdoor recreation, where such operators have been providing adventure (e.g. hunting and fishing) experiences for tourists for some time (at least in North America). The types of experiences of interest to natural resources-based tourists (e.g. adventure tourists and ecotourists) have necessitated the inclusion of businesses that are prepared to offer equipment and other specialised services for tourists. Outfitters, then, are those 'commercial businesses that provide a person with the equipment necessary for an activity or experience' (ibid.: 111). As Tims (1996) implies, outfitting traces its roots back to the early explorers who provided a service to people, usually in a manner that placed humans against nature. More recently, outfitting has progressed to the point where it has taken on professional status trough America Outdoors and the Professional Guide Institute (PGI). The PGI provides training for people in the areas of wild lands heritage back-country leadership. Interpretation, and outfitter operations; with the mission to 'identify, enhance and disseminate the nature interpretive and educational resource of the outfitting industry so that outfitters and guides can offer the highest quality of experience to the public' (ibid.: 177). Clearly, the PGI operates with a mandate that involves guides as a natural ingredient to providing effective back-country experiences.

On a more practical note, an excellent presentation of a hands on approach to ecotourism operation and outfitting is provided by Mitchell (1992). Although this is too detailed to present in its entirely here, he identifies the following main programme-related aspects in structuring and running ecotours: professional tour guiding, a survey of personal assets, a survey of recreational assets, balancing demand, environmental education, tour planning, pricing, preparing the client for the trip, questions clients ask, packing lists, client medical information, cooking and food, conflict resolution, camp and camp cleanliness, first aid, legal considerations, on-the-trail sittings, and evaluation. For those more interested in actually organising and conducting tours, this documents is a must. In addition, more specific guides related to first aid, risk management, leadership, interpretation, recreational programming, marketing and finance, and so on are recommended to prepare the operator for the task of leading successful ventures in the field.

Wilderness tourism and outfitting in the Yukon, Canada A Case Study

The interpretation of ecotourism takes a more general form in the Yukon Territory of Canada. The territory's selection of 'wilderness tourism' as an umbrella term for a variety of different back-country experiences is very much a function of geography (the remote wilderness setting of territory) and the existing products and resources operating in the region. The undeveloped wilderness setting is thus a key factor in the delivery of tourism products in the region. Wilderness tourism is defined as 'tourism related to nature, adventure and culture, which takes place in the "backcountry" and is primarily associated with multi-day trips, although it also includes day tips' (Tompkins 1996). Wilderness tourism is divided into (1) hunting, (2) fishing, and (3) adventure. This latter category is very much a reflection of the adventure tourism definition and activities of the Canadian Tourism Commission. Such activities include nature and wildlife observation, land adventure products, water adventure products, winter adventure products, air adventure products, and native tourism.

Related Research on Operators

One of the earliest papers to emerge on the operation of nature tour companies was written by Ingram and Durst (1989), who designed a study to document empirically the promotion and activities of such companies in the United States. These authors used the Specialty Travel Index to identify 78 tour operators, of which 32 agreed to take part in the study. They concluded that firm size ranged from 20 to 3,000 clients, with three serving over 1,000 clients each. The majority of their client base was described as 'outdoor enthusiasts, retired couples or students, equally male and female, over 30 years old, and usually travelling as individuals in late summer' (ibid.: 12). The companies had been in operation for seven years, on average.

In other reseach, Eagles and Wind (1994) employed a content analysis methodology in analysing the advertising of 347 guide-led ecotours in 50 different countries, most of which were Canadian based. They found that on a average the tours had a guide to participant ratio of about 1:13. This statistic seems to be consistent with the outdoor recreation literature, which recommends guide to participant ratios of approximately 1:12 for hiking (ford and Blanchard 1993). It should be noted that in most cases ecotourism is dependent upon parks and protected areas and those areas' specific guidelines and policies. As such, many parks restrict party sizes to manageable numbers, which means approximately 10 or 12 individuals to a party. The reason for this is not only ecologically based (too much impact on certain areas), but also sociological, in that large groups often contribute to crowding, noise, and other disturbances.

Ecotour operators must be sensitive to such policies, and act accordingly. These potential impacts are well documented in the work of Hendee *et al.* (1990) and Hammitt and Cole (1987). For example, the latter authors suggest that 'large parties are typically defined in wilderness areas as groups larger than 8 to 10 members' (ibid.: 173). Handee et al. (1990: 369) suggest that in most regions, parties with more than 10 individuals account for only about 5 per cent of all groups, and illustrate that party sizes are declining owing to park restrictions and the 'larger, organised groups have generally become smaller as both managers and organisation leaders have become concerned about the impact of large groups on the environment and on other visitors'.

In a survey of 24 North American ecotour operators, Yee (1992) developed a profile of the content and philosophical orientation of such operations. While most (63 per cent) had been in business for 2 to 15 years, 17 per cent had been operating between 15 and 20 years, many suggesting that they were offering ecotours long before the term originated. Ninety-two per cent of respondents followed a code of ethics, and 38 per cent considered ethical conduct in pre-trip orientation; 29 per cent addressed ethics in printed information packs; 13 per cent of those surveyed used videos or slides on ethics; while 33 per cent used lecture formats. The use of trained interpreters and naturalists was also addressed in Yee's research, where it was found that 75 per cent of the respondents had 'ecologists, naturalists or other experts on staff to aid in conducting their tours'.

Researchers have also analysed the degree to which ecotour operators promote and perceive themselves as being environmentally friendly (Weiler 1993). In this study, described as being exploratory, it was found that about 40 per cent of operators were promoted as being environmentally friendly; 66 per cent of operators felt that their tours were either beneficial or very beneficial for the environment (only one was said to be harmful or very harmful); 70 per cent said that their tour educated tourists about impacts; and only 7 per cent said that their tour enhanced the environment through, for example, removing others' rubbish. A companion study (Weiler and Davis 1993) investigated the roles of nature-based tour leaders, and discovered that the main roles of the tour leaders on a five-point scale '(five being most important), on the basis of the responses of the operators, were organiser (mean = 4.6), group leader (4.5), environmental interpreter (4.3), motivator (4.2), teacher (4.0) and entertainer (3.4).

Owing to the nature of the ecotourism experience, tour operators and resource managers have been forced into much closer proximity to each other, which, according to the research of Moore and Carter (1993), has not been a compatible relationship. In an interview of 16 nature-tour operators in Australia, the authors found that from the operators' perspectives, resource managers did not understand aspects of their business, including the profit motive, costs associated with marketing, costs of operations, the motivations and needs of tourists, and the need for minimal infrastructure in remote areas. Conversely, the operators had concerns related to the managers, including the fact that managers did not have a conservations ethic, failed to provide visitors with appropriate information, had little understanding of the need to control visitors, and did not understand resource fragility. These are fundamental differences that exist between the philosophies of the two camps. In particular, the profit motive is one that his not historically been of concern to parks, given park managers' concern for preservation over use. Although not considered in the paper by Moore and Carter, research needs to examine the relationship that exists between the ecotour participant (i.e. the individuals associated with a tour group) and the non-tour participant, especially from the perspective of the park manager. It would be interesting to understand how park managers view tour participants relative to the smaller group or individualised travellers. These authors suggest that a close working relationship must be developed between these two parties in order to meet the objectives of each group.

In a more comprehensive analysis, Higgins (1996) provides an overview of the structure of the nature tourism industry in the United States. In particular, he states that ecotourism is based on the existence of (1) outbound nature tour operators, located in large key cities in industrialised countries; (2) inbound nature tour operators, who are centred in non-industralised countries and usually provide services in one country; and local nature tour businesses, which include hotels, restaurants, ecolodges, souvenirs, guides, and so on. It is the outbound nature tour operators that play the greatest role, according to Higgins, in linking clients with other businesses and destinations around the world, particularly those in non-industrialised countries. In a survey of 82 US nature tour operators, Higgins found that such operations have increased in number by 820 per cent between 1970 and 1994 (from seven to 83) Higgins also discovered that client lists for nature tour operators ranged from 25 to 15,000, with an average of 1,674-35 to which served over 1,000 clients in 1986—with the largest five serving 40 per cent of the total market.

Role of Interpretation

While interpretation is often thought of solely in the context of persons working within parks and protected areas (interpreting the landscape), according to Barrow (1994) interpretation is far more elaborate, and based on three types of planning: (1) town and country, (2) marketing, and (3) education. In the town and country approach, appropriate land use philosophies and techniques are used to protect valuable land from development, provide access to the public, and to help create an affective tie with the resource base. Marketing interpretation, on the other hand, deals with how best to understand various user groups and their particular wants and needs. The marketing approach to interpretation is often product oriented, but must temper this with other concerns of the site (e.g. resource protection). Finally, Barrow suggests that interpretation employs educational theory in its plan development in order to understand how people learn, and what to teach them.

In order to manage effectively, interpretive planners must be sensitive to the learning, behavioural, and emotional sides of interpretation. The I earning Objectives are designed to provide basic topic information or understanding such as: 'The majority of the visitors will be able to describe three reasons why protecting archeological sites benefits all visitors.' But the real—or most important-aim the manager may have in mind for interpretation to accomplish is to prevent visitors from picking up 'souvenirs' such as pottery shards at archaeological sites. So the Behavioural objective might be: 'All visitors will leave alone any artifacts that they may find at the site and not to take them home.' It is the job of the Emotional objectives for the interpreter to get the visitors to appreciate the value of artifacts left in place, and fell that they are doing a good thing by not removing anything. So an objective of this kind might be: 'The majority of visitors will feel a sense of responsibility for not touching any artifacts they may find on the ground'.

The behaviour is the action that the interpreter would like to occur as a result of the interpretive programme: whereas the emotional objective prompts the interpreter to strive to realise how best to get the visitor to feel as though he or she is behaving in the appropriate manner at the site and beyond; that is, that the behaviour is something that they should want to do. Veverka illustrates that the same philosophy is used by advertisers today, that they make you feel as though you want or need a particular product.

The behavioural response is to actually go out and purchase a product.

Interpretation, as identified earlier by Weiler and Davis (1993), plays a significant role in the delivery of ecotourism services. For example, on Great Barrier Reef Marine Park in Australia Hockings (1994) examined the tour operator's role in marine park interpretation. While staff-recreationist interactions are not very high as a consequence of the level of use and size of the park, tourists have come to rely on the various tour operators in securing information. Of a sample of 170 operators, 72 per cent of respondents indicated offering interpretation as part of their programme. A higher proportion of this number were found to be day reef trip, diving, and sailing operators; while a lower percentage of fishing operators provided interpretation. A significant finding of the study was that 56 per cent of staff involved in interpretation had no relevant formal qualifications, while only 4 per cent of all staff had formal qualifications. It was suggested that this overall lack of training could not be linked to type to activity offered (types of activities included scenic flights, fishing, camping, day reef trip, seaplane rides, dive trips, and so on), as those indicated as having the appropriate interpretive qualifications were evenly spread across operator types and sizes. Operators, according to Hockings, relied more on practical experience as a means by which to inform clients.

Forestell (1993) has developed a unique model of interpretation and environmental education that he operationalised in his work in whalewatching. This author suggests that tourists experience different cognitive states during a whalewatching excursion that require the naturalist/interpreter to articulate information in three distinct periods; pre-contact withwhales, contact, and post-contact. Pre-contact information involves learning on how participants should interact with the whales. This may be supplemented with geographical information and marine environmental education. In the second, or contact, stage, interpreters focus on the need for participants to seek answers to a variety of questions related to the observation of the animals. Questions typically relate to whale identification, whale behaviour, verification of knowledge, and safety. The goal of this stage is to 'generate motivation to learn by creating or uncovering and imbalance between an individual's initial knowledge base, and some current perception of the world..[and] provide sound knowledge to allow the participant to regain cognitive balance'(Forestell 1993: 274). The final stage, post-contact, is characterised by the participants need to make pre-and post-trip comparisons of whales and the marine world, and in addition to consider broader environmental issues (including active and financial support for conservation programmes or issues). Clients also question leaders about the well-being of the whales. Forestell suggests that ecotourism experience has the ability to empower people to synthesise unscientific observation with scientific fact, which he feels is not an inferior substitute for hard data, but rather one that is experiential and practical. This model demonstrates the need for interpreters to be sensitive to the different stages of an ecoturism experience. In situations where guides are providing more personal knowledge of a setting only, Forestell perhaps would argue for more of a trained approach to the delivery of the interpretive product, which would ultimately enable the tourist to benefit further from the experience.

Ecotourism has blossomed into a rich a array of programmes and opportunities in the public, private, and not-for-profit sectors. Often a relationship must exist between public agencies (those who manage parks and protected areas) and private operators (those who run programmes in these public spaces). Good coordination must exist between these stakeholders such that the appropriate values (economic and emotional) are attached to the ecotourism experience.

Bibliography

Allcock, A, Jones, B., Lane S., & Grant J. (1994), National Ecotourism Strategy, Canberra, ACT: Commonwealth Department of Tourism.

Allison, Lyn. (1998), Access to Heritage: User charges in museums, art galleries and national parks. Report of the Senate Environment, Recreation, Communications & the Arts References Committee, Parliament of the commonwealth of Australia: Canberra.

Arato, Andrew, 2000, *Civil Society, Constitution, and Legitimacy*, Lanham Md.: Rowman & Littlefield.

Australian Nature Conservation Agency (1995). *Kangaroo Harvesting*. Canberra: ANCA.

Baker, Gideon, 2002, *Civil Society and Democratic Theory: Alternative Voices*. London: Rutledge.

Benjamin, Barer R. 1999. "Clansmen, Consumers, and Citizens: Three Takes on Civil Society," In Robert K. Fullinwider, ed., *Civil Society, Democracy, and Civic Renewal*. Lanham, Md.: Roman & Littlefield.

Berman, Sheri, 2001. "Civil Society and Political Institutionalisation." In Bob Edwards, Michael W. Foley, and Mario Diani, eds., *Beyond Tocqueville: Civil Society and the Social Capital Debate in Comparative Perspective*. Hanover, N.H.: University Press of New England.

Bermeo, Nancy, 2000. "Civil Society after Democracy: Some Conclusions." In Nancy Bermeo and Phillip Nord, eds., *Civil Society Before Democracy: Lessons from Nineteenth Century Europe*, Lanham, Md.: Rowman & Littlefield.

Bratton, Michael. 1994. "Civil Society and Political Transitions in Africa," In John W. Harbeson, Donald Rothchild, and Naomi Chazan, eds., *Civil Society and the State in Africa*, Boulder: Lynne Rienner.

Briguglio, L., Butler, R.W., Harrison, D. and Filho. W.L. (1996) *Sustainable Tourism in Islands and Small States: Case Studies*, London: Pinter.

Butynski, T,M., & Kalina, J. (1998). Gorilla Tourism: A critical look. In I.J. Guilland, & R. Mace (Eds)., *Conservation of Biological Resources* (pp. 294-313). Oxford: Blackwell Science.

Cohen, Jean L., and Andrew Arato. 1992. *Civil Society and Political Theory*. Cambridge, Mass.: MIT Press.

Commission for Environmental Cooperation (1999). *The development of sustainable tourism in natural areas in North America*: Background, issues and opportunities. Discussion Paper (pp. 27-28), Cancum, Mexico.

Commonwealth Australia (1996). *National Strategy for the Conservation of Australia's Biological Diversity*. Canberra: Imprint Limited.

Cox, Robert W. 1999. "Civil Society at the Turn of the Millennium: Prospects for an Alternate World Order." *Review of International Studies* 25(1):3-29.

Cronin, L. (2000). *Key Guide to Australian Mammals* (Revised Edition). Annandale, NSW: Envirobook.

Diamond, Larry. 1999. *Developing Democracy: Toward Consolidation* Baltimore: Johns Hopkins University Press.

Dredge, D. (1999). Destination place, planning and design. *Animals of Tourism Research,* 26 (4), 772-792.

Edington, J.M. (1986). *Ecology, Recreation and tourism.* Cambridge: Press Syndicate of the University of Cambridge.

Edwards, Bob, and Michael W. Foley, 2001. "Civil Society and Social Capital: A Primer," In Bob Edwards, Michael W. Foley, and Mario Diani, eds., *Beyond Tocqueville: Civil Society and the Social Capital Debate in Comparative Perspective,* Hanover, N.H.: University Press of New England.

Edwards, Bob, Michael W. Foley, and Mario Diani, eds. 2001. *Beyond Tocqueville: Civil Society and the Social Capital Debate in Comparative Perspective.* Hanover, N.H. University Press of New England.

Ferguson, Adam, (1767) 1995, *An Essay on the History of Civil Society.* Edited by Fania Oz Salzberger. Cambridge: Cambridge University Press.

Fine, Robert. 1997. "Civil Society: Theory Enlightenment, and Critique" In Robert Fine and Shirin Rai, eds., *Civil Society: Democratic Perspectives.* London: Frank Cass.

Foley, Michael, W., and Bob Edwards, 1997. "Escape from Politics? Social Theory and Social Capital Discourse." *American Behavioral Scientist* 40(5): 550—61.

Freese, C. (1996). *The commercial, consumptive use of wild species: Managing it for the benefit of biodiversity.* Discussion, Paper, WWF US and WWF International.

Freese, C. (1998). *Wild Species as Commodities: Managing Markets and Ecosystems for Sustainability.* Washington, D.C.: Island Press.

Gellner, Ernest, 1994. *Conditions of Liberty: Civil Siciety and its Rivals,* New York; Penguin Books.

Gilbert, D.C. (1990) 'Conceptual issues in the meaning of tourism.' In Copper, C.P. (ed.) *Progress in Tourism, Recreation and Hospitality Management*, Vol. 2, London: Belhaven: 4-27.

Green, R., & Higginbottom, K. (2000). The effects of non-consumptive wildlife tourism on free-ranging wildlife: A Review. *Pacific Conservation Biology*, 6,183-197.

Gunderson, H.L. (1976) *Mammalogy*, New York: McGraw-Hill Book Company.

Holmes, J.C. (1976). Parasites as threats to biodiversity in shrinking ecosystems. *Biodiversity and Conservation*, 5, 975-983.

Hudock, Ann C. 1999. *NGOs and Civil Society: Democracy* by Proxy. Cambride: Polity Press.

Hunter, C. and Green, H. (1995) *Tourism and the Environment : A sustainable Relationship*?, London: Routledge.

Ioannidou, Anastasia, 1997. "The Politics of the Divison of Labour: Smith and Hegel on Civil Society." In Robert Fine and Shirin Rai, eds, *Civil Society: Democratic Perspectives*. London: Frank Cass.

Kaviraj, Sudipta, and Sunil Khilnani, eds., 2001. *Civil Society: History and Possibilities*, Cambridge: Cambridge University Press.

Matheieson, A. and Wall, G. (1982) *Tourism Economic. Physical and Social Impacts*, Harlow: Longman.

Mitchell, L.S. and Murphy, P.E. (1991) 'Geography and tourism,' *Annas of Tourism Research*, Vol. 18 No. 1:57-70.

Moore, K., Cushman, G. and Simmons, D. (1995) 'Behavioural conceptualisations of tourism and leisure', *Annals of Tourism Research*, Vol. 22 No. 1: 67-75.

Murphy, P.E. (1985) *Tourism—A Community Approach*, London:

Routledge.

Nord, Phillip. 2000. "Introduction," In Nancy Bermeo and Philip Nord, eds., *Civil Society Before Democracy: Lessons from Nineteenth Century Europe.* Lanham, Md.: Rowman & Littlefield.

Pearce, P.L. (1993) 'Fundamentals to Tourist Motivation'. In Pearce, D.G. and Butler, R.W. (eds.) *Tourism Research,* London: Routledge: 113-134.

Pearce, D. (1987) *Tourism Today: A Geographical Analysis,* Harlow: Longman.—(1989) *Tourism Development,* Harlow: Longman.

Shaw, G. and Williams, A.M. (1994) *Critical Issues in Tourism.- A Geographical Perspective,* Oxford.

Smith, V.L. and Eadington, W.R. (eds) (1994) *Tourism Alternatives: Potentials and Problems in the Development of Tourism,* London: John Wiley.

Smith, R.V. and Mitchell, L.S. (1990) 'Geography and tourism: a review of selected literature'. In Cooper, C.P. (ed.) *Progress in Tourism, Recreation and Hospitality Management.* Vol.2, London: Belhaven: 50-66.

Stepan, Alfred, 1988. *Rethinking Military Politics: Brazil and the Southern Cone,* Princeton: Princeton University Press.

Theobald, W. (1994) 'The context, meaning and scope of tourism' in Theobald, W. (ed.) *Global Tourism: The Next Decade,* Oxford; Butterworth Heinemann: 3-19.

Warren, Mark E. 2001. *Democracy and Association.* Princeton: Princeton University Press.

Index

A

Aberdeen and Grampian Tourism Board (AGTB), 138

Adventure Tourism, 19

Adventure Products, 20

Annapurna Conservation Area in Nepal, 69

Angus & Dundee Tourist Board (ADTB), 138

Australian Tourism Operations Association, 37

B

Ballantine, 13

Bicycling and Hiking, 110

C

Cairngorms Tourism Market, 139

Canoes and Kayaks, 109

Canadian Forestry Service, 5

Costa Rica, 77

D

Durst and Laarman, 7

E

EEA, 59

Eagles, 13

Ecotourism Guidelines for Nature Tour Operators, 42

Economic Impact and Employment, 119

Environmental Impacts and Nature Tourism, 68

Evaluation and Monitoring of Ecotourism, 33-67

Evaluation of Local Accommodations, 42

F

Fennell, 5

Fillion, Foley, 172

Forestell, 253

G

Gardner, 244

German Primte Centrer, 133

Great Texas Coastal Birding Trail, 9

Green Evaluations Project, 39

Green Evaluation Survey, 59

Geographical Positioning Systems, 214

Geographical Information System, 214

Goodwin, 10

Goodale and Cater, 35

H

Hall, 20

Hawkins in Giannecchini, 219

Higgins, 4

Highlands of Scotland Tourist Board (HOST), 138

Hiller, 38

Hunting and Wildlife-Associated Recreation, 106

I

IMPLAN, 116, 117

Information and Education, 42

International Trends in Nature Tourism, 207-217

K

Kaye, 13

L

Laarman and Gregersen, 184

Lindberg, 77

Lingkungan, 133

M

McBektm 68

Monteverde Cloud Forest Biological Preserve, 77

Miller and Kaye, 13

N

Nature Tourism, Motivation, 25

Nature Tourism and culture, 87

National Sruvey of Fishing, 106

Non-environemntal Organisation, 132

O

Ocean City, 87

Ontario's Algonquin Provincial Park, 177

Opportunities of Nature Tourism, 1

P

Pre-Departure Information, 42

Professional Social Accounting and Impact Analysis, 116

Psysiological and psychological needs, 25

Q

Queesland Department of the Environment, 187

R

RV camping, 185

Ryan, 238

S

Skills and challenge, 21

Socio-demographic Information About Ecotourist, 42, 45

SWOT, 142

T

TIES, 40, 41, 42

Travel Scope, 105

Tourism Destinations, 2

Tourism Marketing Strategy, 135

Tourist Typologies, 24

Tour Operator Contributions to Conservation and Local Development Programmes, 42

V

Visitor Impact Management and Visitor Experiece Resource Protection, 77

Visitor Survey, 109

W

Wallance, 11

Wells, 175, 176

Y

Year Round Destination, 141

Yellowstone, 7

Z

Ziffer, 11

***